Dynamic BellyDance

Here's more praise for:

Dynamic BellyDance

The Joyful Journey of Dancemaking and Performing:

"Wow, a zero to 60 bellydance experience! Enjoyable for everyone, even a truly new beginner." —Sheryl Parsons, actress at the New American Shakespeare Tavern (Atlanta, Georgia)

"Ramona, I've just read your book, which I enjoyed very much . . . I thought it was very clear and well written, with lots of good, practical advice." —Wendy Buonaventura, author of *Serpent of the Nile* (London, England)

"I really enjoyed reading this book and think it will help dancers who are approaching choreographing their dances . . . Your book drew me in and I engaged in a 'conversation.' . . . Well done!" —Andrea Deagon, Ph.D., dancer and instructor (North Carolina)

"The content of the book is perfect . . ." —Hilary Thacker, dancer and instructor (Edinburgh, Scotland)

"I enjoyed it immensely . . . Dynamic BellyDance *is interesting and informative."* —Saroya, dancer and instructor (Atlanta, Georgia)

"Ramona, what a great book you've written. It's articulate, informative and easy to read and understand." —Satinka, dancer (Atlanta, Georgia)

"Good approaches for creating choreographed dances. I enjoyed this!" —Christine, dancer (Seattle, Washington)

"Ramona, you have done a wonderful job! It is clearly well written and I am happy to say that I learned quite a bit reading it." —Marshall Lewis, Registered Masters Level Psychologist (Kansas)

"Ramona, Dynamic BellyDance *exquisitely conveys your enthusiasm for performance, which will inspire students and other dancers to tweak their presentations."* —Tony Rutherford, Huntington News Net reporter (West Virginia)

Dynamic BellyDance

The Joyful Journey of
Dancemaking and Performing

Ramona

AMERICAN BELLYDANCE INNOVATIONS

ATLANTA, GA

Published by
American Bellydance Innovations
P.O. Box 1083
Atlanta, GA 30301-1083

Attention dance instructors, colleges, universities, and magazine publishers:
Quantity discounts are available on bulk purchases of this book for educational
training purposes, fund-raising, or gift giving. Magazine publishers: book excerpts
can be created to fit your specific needs. For more information, email
Ramona@DynamicBellyDance.com.

While the author and publisher have made every effort to provide accurate internet
addresses at the time of publication, neither the author nor the publisher assume
any responsibility for errors and changes that occur after publication. Further,
the publisher does not have any control over and does not assume any
responsibility for third-party websites or their content.

Library of Congress Cataloging in Publication Data available upon request
ISBN-13: 978-0-615-13326-3
ISBN-10: 0-615-13326-6

Book Design and Production by Studio 31
www.studio31.com

Cover and frontispiece photos of Ramona on Jekyll Island, Georgia
by Beautiful Photos, Inc.

Printed in China

Disclaimer

Consult your doctor or trusted medical practitioner before beginning any exercise program. Never force or strain during dancing. While extensive research has been done to
assure accuracy of the information herein, the author of this book disclaims any liability or loss in connection with the exercises and advice herein. It is the author's hope
that this book will help you to determine for yourself the practices that are most
appropriate for your own body. We believe that self-knowledge and self-responsibility
will ultimately make these types of disclaimers unnecessary. Peace to all.

Contents

Part IV: Music and Dance

Part V: Students, Teachers and Audiences

Acknowledgments

I've benefitted from conversations and classes with many knowledgeable dancers and instructors. Without their insight and willingness to share, this book wouldn't be possible.

My deep appreciation and thanks to Wendy Buonaventura, Dr. Andrea Deagon, Carolena Nericcio, Saroya of Atlanta, Hilary Thacker, Satinka, Sheryl Parsons, Delilah, Christine Hamby and Marshall Lewis for their valuable feedback on the draft manuscript.

I am also deeply grateful to the dancers and photographers who provided their photographs for inclusion in this book. Additional thank-yous to Elisheba Zoheret and to all the dancers who gave me title suggestions.

The following dancers inspired me during classes, workshops, conversations, correspondence and/or private instruction. Thank you for sharing your expertise so generously with me and other dancers over the years: Carolena Nericcio, Suhaila Salimpour, Yasmina Ramzy, Delilah, Cassandra, LaRue Mangelly, Kalila, Diana of Atlanta, Aegela, Valerie Larkin, Fahtiem, Suzanna del Vecchio, Morocco, Jillina, Amaya, Bert Balladine, Dalia, Hilary Thacker, Fereshteh Hosseini, Oracle, Tandi, Aspyn, Julena, Saroya, Zhaleh Fereshteh, Beata and Horacio Cifuentes, Aziz, Aziza, Ragia Hassan, Hadia, Mahmoud Reda, Mohammed Khalil, Nagwa Fouad, and the late Ibrahim Farrah. The musicians of Sirocco, and percussion instructors Layne Redmond, Daveed and Sylvanis also gave me inspiration.

Special thanks to all the dance students who've taken my group classes and studied privately; your feedback has been invaluable. Thanks to my mother for sending me to dance lessons when I was very young.

And last, but not least, thank-you to my wonderful husband Jack and son Andrew, who support me in all my projects and give me the benefit of their observations and insight.

A Personal Prologue

Throughout 20 years of studying belly dance, various instructors gave me tips and hints about creating choreography from time to time. Information about how to design a dance was discussed as an aside to learning dance technique and choreographed dances.

Some tips I received were: *"use different floor patterns for variety," "let's change direction,"* and *"stopping all movement for a few seconds is a good dramatic accent."* When I asked one of America's top belly dancers about her method of creating choreographed dances, she replied, *"I listen to the music, and it* [the choreography] *just comes."* When I asked other top dancers the same question, I received similar answers.

I reached a frustration point in my dance career when I realized that although I'd mastered a repertoire of dance movements, combining them into a choreographed dance was difficult and time-consuming. I was not alone in my frustration; a fellow instructor told me she spent 40 hours creating just one choreography of about five minutes duration.

Improvised dances were easier for me, but I felt uncomfortable with the way they turned out. I was learning ever more complex movements in technique classes and workshops, but I didn't know what to do with the movements when class was over. Around this time, I'd also begun noticing that some of the best dances I'd seen also had the simplest movements.

The choreography classes I'd attended were group exercises for creating a dance to a specific song. I was frustrated because those classes didn't teach me how to create a dance to *any* piece of music. So I went to the library to find answers in dance literature.

OPPOSITE: *The author in costume.*

Choreography and improvisation

I searched old magazine archives and books, and talked to other dancers, but I could not find information in print or elsewhere about how to create belly dance choreography. There seemed to be no information about how to combine belly dance movements into an organized and meaningful dance.

Some talented belly dance choreographers are paid by other professional dancers to create choreographies for performances. Many dancers create their own choreography, and also dance well by using improvisation. Some dancers prefer the feeling of dancing by improvisation, although they are skilled choreographers.

Dancing by improvisation is a choice for some dancers, who embrace and enjoy the experience of improvisation. For others, it is a default approach because they have difficulty creating choreography. A few of the performers I spoke with have such a challenge with creating choreography that they said, *"I always improv."*

Some instructors said they use ready-made choreographies they learn from other dancers at workshops or from DVDs, in order avoid the time-consuming process of creating their own dances. Some told me that they create choreography sometimes, but that it takes an excessive and frustrating amount of time.

Improvisation is appropriate in many situations. At parties, restaurant performances, with live musicians and at informal functions, it is the method of choice and very appropriate. Yet improvisation is also a vital skill necessary for creating choreography. Though many people think of belly dance as traditionally improvisational, professional dancers of the Near East have used both choreography and improvisation skills for many years.

Modern belly dancers all over the world use choreography extensively in theatrical and staged performances. Having a scripted routine enables performers to excel during stage performances. One instructor remarked that using choreographies for her American Tribal belly dance troupe was "less exhausting" than improvising every performance.[1] This is an interesting comment, since Tribal style is generally associated with group improvisation.

Choreography and improvisation work hand in hand. Improvisational skill is crucial to professional-level performance, but good improvisation also requires many skills central to choreographing dances: understanding the way music is organized, the relationship of movement to music, and using a theme and motifs.

Dancemaking demystified

Since the information I wanted was not available in printed belly dance literature, I researched the dance literature of modern and jazz dance genres. I found helpful information about how to choreograph and improvise dances. However, these references lacked specific insight into belly dance. Creating belly dance routines has factors in common with creating dances in other dance forms, although belly dance is unique in its music, movements, stylization, and history.

I started applying what I'd learned about dancemaking from other genres to the dances I was creating for belly dance solos and group performances. During this process, I made several discoveries. Though it took time and I went through a learning curve in creating dances, before long I could create good dances with much *less* time and effort than before. Understanding the structure of songs and using a theme and motifs makes creating dances easier.

My students liked the dances better, and my students, fellow performers and instructors complimented me on my choreographies and improvisations. Students learned the dances faster, and

I was happier with my teaching. It became easier for me to develop dances for my students, and I was gaining more satisfaction from teaching and performances.

I felt that others who were seeking help with belly dance choreography might benefit from this knowledge, and so I started writing this book.

Exploration of dance creativity

Creative expression is a continuing quest, and, though my dances are getting better, I still have a long way to go. To improve our self-expression, we need to try new things. Failure is always a key component of success in *any* creative process. It took Thomas Edison literally thousands of tries before he was successful in inventing the light bulb, and most novelists have books which were rejected before they publish a bestseller. During any creative process we usually find out what *does not* work before we find out what *does* work. All creative efforts have their risks and rewards, and require innovative thinking and new insight.

Learning about choreographic and improvisational elements, good dance technique, and presentation skills will enhance the delivery of your performance to the audience, and is useful in teaching dance classes. Whether you choose to dance by spontaneously improvising or by scripting your dances in advance, I hope this book helps you in your quest.

PART ONE

SETTING THE SCENE

OPPOSITE: *Coco in her studio.*

INTRODUCTION

What makes a great dance?

"Dance is an ancient form of magic."

HEINRICH ZIMMER (1890–1943), GERMAN-AMERICAN AUTHOR

*H*ow do you define a great belly dance routine? I like the simple definition one of my first belly dance teachers gave: *A good dance is one that the audience enjoys and which holds its attention.*

No matter how much or how little training an audience has with dance, it's very easy to see the difference between a dance that shows the dancer's skill, and one that does not. Yet it isn't easy to define *specifically* what makes a dance great. If it were so simple, we would all be great dancers!

Magical moments

Although I've seen many wonderful dances, there have been only a few times in my life that I've seen dances that really moved me, that spoke to my soul. There was something indefinable and magic about those performances, and the dancers who performed them. I felt carried away into a state of enchantment while watching them. (Arabic audiences call this feeling *tarab*.) These magical performances motivated me to find out what that special "something extra" was that made their performances stir such emotion in their audiences.

What then, technically, makes a dance great? The common traits that great dance performers have in common are:

- *Technical skill,*
- *Meaningful choreography,*
- *Strong improvisational skills,*
- *Powerful emotional expression,* and
- *Presentation skills.*

OPPOSITE: *Dancing is a powerful form of nonverbal communication, as well as being entertaining. Lamis performing in Orlando, Florida. (Photo courtesy of JAPHO Photography and Jeff Mischke.)*

Meaningful choreography, heightened improvisational skills, and emotional expression are more elusive than technical skill. With technique, you can explain a step and teach someone how to do it. However, it is more difficult to explain and teach someone self-expression through movement, and great improvisational and choreographed belly dance is inextricably linked with emotional expression. Master choreographer Ibrahim (Bobby) Farrah used to say that *dances begin where learning steps ends.*[2]

When asked why women particularly preferred her style of Oriental dance, the late Egyptian dancer Tahaya Carioca replied, *"I was praying, not dancing."* This comment reflects the meditative, expressive quality of belly dance, the dancing from the heart which "speaks" nonverbally to women.

Presentation skills refer to "stage presence" and the "delivery" of the dance to the audience: the ability to be at ease and project personality and emotion. This aspect of dance is related to the skills that an actress uses to deliver her lines. The skilled dancer not only performs her steps with technical skill, but also uses her facial expression, posture, eye contact and other "soft skills" to communicate with the audience. Just as voice coaches train actresses in how to deliver lines, dance teachers also coach their students in presentation skills.

Dance as communication

To truly excel as dancers, we must understand that the act of dancing is a powerful form of *nonverbal communication.* You are showing the audience something profoundly personal about yourself every time you dance.

In everyday life, you see an indication of individual personalities by the way people dress, their physical characteristics, facial expressions and the way they move. On the stage, our dress and costume preferences show our audiences whether we like to dress conservatively or be trendy, what colors and jewelry styles we like, and how understated, fashionable or flashy we like to be. Our bodies display our physical fitness level, muscular coordination, and even our nutritional and exercise habits. Our entire bodies, and particularly our hands and face, express our emotions.

Beyond this, the movements we select and the way we choose to organize them shows the audience something about our creative ability: how shy or outgoing we are, our level of athletic ability and artistic sense, our comfort level with expressing emotions, how organized we are, how comfortable we are in front of an audience, and a myriad of other personal traits. All these factors are an integral part of dance, inseparable from the dancer.

In novels and plays, the plot is also inseparable from the characters. The main character is driving the plot, and the plot is driving the main character; they are interdependent. It is the same with dance. A dance consisting of exquisitely performed movements, but without the dancer's personality, heartfelt emotions and plot (sequence of meaningful movements) tells us *nothing.* However, a dancer who puts her personality into simple movements with skill, energy, motivation, highlights and climactic points, "speaks" to us in a nonverbal, abstract language.

There is always one person in the audience to whom you speak

The dances we see speak to us. Our involvement may be on a superficial level, simply receiving entertainment, but sometimes we may see something in a performance which moves us into a deeply personal emotion. Sometimes an insightful recognition of a profound truth comes into our awareness.

Dance is again like language; the conversations we have with the people in our lives vary daily,

*There is always one person in the audience to whom you speak. Ramona and
The Gwinnett Belly Dancers in an Atlanta performance.*

from the mundane to the deeply meaningful conversations. A conversation or a dance can unex-
pectedly turn into something profound.

Immediately following one performance of
Martha Graham's modern interpretive dance
Lamentation, a woman from the audience told
Martha, *"You will never know what you have done for
me tonight. Thank you."*[3] The woman had lost her
son in a tragic accident, but had been unable to
express her grief. Seeing *Lamentation* was therapeutic for her.

Martha Graham said, *"What I learned that night is
that there is always one person in the audience to whom
you speak. One."*[4] Martha Graham later performed
the same dance at a different theater, and received
a completely different reaction from that other
audience. Every individual is unique, and so is
every audience.

Sometimes, a dance performance will profoundly touch us and bring a new recognition of

something into our lives . . . something important,
but which cannot be expressed with merely words.
This is communication in its most elemental
sense.[5]

Enhancing the great dance moves you already know

In this book, we will explore the technical skills of
choreography and improvisation. I am assuming
that you already know, at a minimum, basic belly
dancing movements. This book is about how to
take the dance skills you already have, and use
them to create innovative and expressive dances.
Whether you know five steps or five hundred
steps, the how-to's of making dances are the
same.

Choreography and improvisation are a unique
expression of *you*.

For your contemplation:

Inspiration: What do you remember most about a dance performance you liked? What were your impressions of the performer's personality? Her dance technique? If you have a recording of one of your own performances, watch the recording, then ask yourself these same questions from the point of view of an audience member.

Role model: Who is the dancer that most inspires you? Reflect on what it is about her that resonates with you. What qualities does she have that you identify with? Do you have characteristics (body type, facial expressions, gesture habits, costume style preferences) in common with her? What qualities of this role model do you want to develop within yourself? What characteristics and qualities do you already have that you would like to highlight or develop?

Preferences: Do you prefer to dance using choreography, or by improvising? For what reason? When you see dance performances by other artists, do you prefer to see choreography or improvisation? Do you sense when a performer is improvising or dancing choreography? Do you like it best when you can't tell whether it's spontaneous or improvised?

Best performances: Have you seen or performed in a dance which felt more fulfilling or made you feel happier than other performances? What made that performance outstanding? What feelings did you experience during and after the performance? (One way of creating dances is to reflect on the feelings that came out of a previous dance, then meditate about those feelings and let dance movements emerge spontaneously.)

20

CHAPTER ONE

Choreography and Improvisation

"Dance is a universal language."

NAGWA FOUAD, EGYPT'S "QUEEN OF ORIENTAL DANCE"

A great belly dance performance appears effortless. It looks, feels, and sounds like interaction between the dancer, the music, *and* the audience. As the performer, you feel the music in your gut, your feet, your soul and every part of your being, and you take the audience with you on your journey.

"If good choreography looks spontaneous, why do I need to know how to create choreography? Why not improvise all the time?"

If you were to give a speech in front of a large group of people, would you do a better job speaking "off the cuff," or by preparing a speech in advance? Presidents, politicians, and public speakers employ the skills of professional speech writers (who choreograph words) because they express their ideas more eloquently if they *prepare in advance* for their high-profile public appearances.

Everyone who speaks has a native language and an accent, showing her origin. For dancers, our nonverbal "language" is our style. We call our dances by many different names: *Oriental, Egyptian cabaret, Turkish cabaret, Raqs sharqi (Dance of the East), folkloric, American cabaret belly dance, American Tribal Style (ATS), tribal fusion, old style, modern Egyptian, Lebanese,* or other descriptive terms. Just as each of us has a unique voice with an accent and distinctive verbal patterns, each of us also has a distinctive style of dance.

As dancers, we have the challenge of effectively showing our ideas about movement in front of large and small audiences, in public appearances such as dance concerts, charity shows, and on television. Formal settings such as these are good opportunities to present choreographed dances, to show our skills to our best advantage.

While belly dancing is traditionally associated with improvisation and informal settings, performers have also been using choreography in theater performances and stage shows for many years. Professional performers in old times depended upon showing their best skills to their patrons to earn a dependable income, just as dancers do today.

Preparing in advance gives you the opportunity to try out your ideas, so that you can give your best possible presentation. Choreography is a plan for eloquent communication through dance.

Like any good public speaker or performer, you may also include spontaneous elements in your choreography to express yourself better, and to respond to the individualities of a particular audience. Creating choreography is a stepping stone to building better improvisational skills, and vice-versa.

"How will improvisation help me dance better?"

Improvisation is an essential tool in constructing choreography. We improvise to "try out" movements, to find out whether they are a good "fit" with the music, and when the movements don't fit, we then select others.

Improvisation is an essential skill when you have the benefit of dancing with a live band. It's also wonderful for impromptu or informal settings, such as at restaurants and birthday parties. Like situations which require "off the cuff" speeches, there are many situations where a dancer wants to be totally spontaneous.

Choreography and improvisation are closely related skills. By developing choreography skills, your improvisation skills will grow, and vice versa. Choreography means planning your movements; improvisation means spontaneously moving. Both skills are important to a dancer, and both require understanding music, rhythm, and dance technique.

"Who wants choreography?"

"Beginners want *dances*," Atlanta instructor Saroya once told me.

This means that beginner students want to feel a sense of accomplishment after a session of

OPPOSITE: *A choreographed folkloric cane dance by Saroya in an Atlanta theater.*

classes. A short dance routine gives them confidence that they can perform a complete dance, and it helps them remember the movements they learned. It also gives them a ready-made routine that they can perform for their family and friends, and for their own enjoyment.

Beginners are not the only ones who want dances. Many intermediate and advanced workshops also focus on teaching choreographed dances to introduce innovative movements and advanced technical skills. Choreography also acts as a bridge, to show examples of how to link different movements into artistically pleasing combinations. Combinations are short, planned sets of movements, which are mini-choreographies (*choreographic phrases*) within a dance.

Technique classes without choreography tend to be geared toward intermediate and advanced level students who are seeking new ways to explore isolated movements, and who already possess some level of choreography and improv skills.

"What types of performances are there?"

There is more than one kind of performance. There are performances for audiences at festivals, concerts, parties, talent shows, and also performances in which we dance for ourselves, without an audience, and, perhaps, without anyone else being in the same room. This is different from practice, because "practice" is working on something specific to attempt to improve it. Dancing for self-enjoyment is like watercolor painting for relaxation, or sketching for pleasure, or meditating. It's a way of reducing stress and nurturing ourselves.

Another focus of Near Eastern dance is dancing informally, at social events such as wedding showers or other ladies-only celebrations, and at *haflas* (parties). At these events, while others may be watching us, we're not really dancing for them.

Belly dance is not confined to women only. Throughout this book dancers are referred to as "she," since the majority of dancers are women.

A contemporary sword dance by Ramona in an Atlanta restaurant.

For your contemplation:

Comfort level: Do you feel more comfortable performing planned dance routines, or dancing by improvisation? How do you feel emotionally and physically after dancing either of these styles? What things could you do (or already are doing) to feel more comfortable with dancing the style which seems more difficult to you?

Performances: Is public performance a goal or a regular activity for you? If so, where do you feel most comfortable performing? Is one performance venue more comfortable than another? Why? How does your dancing differ when you are alone, versus when you're with others in a classroom or on a stage? Are you more comfortable in front of certain audiences?

Audience interaction: During a recent dance concert in Atlanta, a toddler in the front row was bouncing up and down on her mother's lap while a soloist was dancing. This caught the eye of the dancer on the stage, and she focused on the toddler and mirrored the child's bouncing by bouncing on her own heels for a few seconds. Then, she redirected her focus and smoothly continued her dance.

The moment between the dancer and the toddler was a fun interlude. It was also an example of one of the ways a dancer may interact with her audience, injecting spontaneity into a choreographed performance.

Do you make eye contact, speak with, or otherwise interact with the audience when performing? Do you prefer to be more reserved and set apart from the audience? What ideas or habits do you have when interacting with audiences?

For the sake of simplicity, this term includes all dancers. However, more American men are joining belly dance classes and troupes, and men also have a long tradition of dance in the Eastern world. Some of the most inspiring performers and instructors in this genre are men.

CHAPTER TWO

Posture, Breath and Energy

"The only limits there are, are the limits we put on ourselves."

VALERIE LARKIN, BELLY DANCE PERFORMING AND TEACHING ARTIST, DUBLIN, IRELAND

*E*nergy level in belly dance is all about showing how the music makes you *feel*. In everyday life when we're energetic, we walk briskly, and show this feeling by our individual characteristics, such as posture, breathing pattern, facial expression, speech, and more. When we're tired, we walk slowly, drag our feet, and show our tiredness through other individual physical characteristics. We shiver if we're cold, complain if we're hot, turn pale if we feel ill. Our eyes light up and our whole posture perks up if we feel interested in something. In dance, we physically show our unique physical and personal response to a piece of music and a step.

What is good posture?

The best and easiest method I've found for assessing and maintaining good posture came from a chiropractor. At a bookstore event, the chiropractor offered a "free assessment" to advertise his practice. The "free assessment" was simply taking a side-view photograph of the person and seeing whether their ear, shoulder, and hip were in alignment. He then showed the photograph to the prospective customer, and prescribed chiropractic treatments for those with posture misalignments.

People who spend a lot of time sitting at a desk tend to let their head come forward, ahead of the shoulders. This is particularly noticeable on some college students and advanced degree graduates. The forward position of the head creates a chain reaction of effects down the body. The chiropractor told me that the ear, shoulder, and hip should be in alignment when standing in the neutral stance. This information is in some dance reference books too.

There are small variations in healthy posture; correct alignment varies due to individual anatomy, because the back is uniquely structured in each person.[6] Basic dance posture also varies depending on the style of the belly dance (for

Posture in alignment: ear, shoulder, hip and center of foot in alignment, knees relaxed. Correct alignment varies due to individual anatomy.

Posture out of alignment: head thrust forward, slumped shoulders, shortened lower back, knees locked. This unhealthy posture would lead to painful consequences over time.

example, cabaret posture, tribal posture and Turk-ish posture are not the same), but all styles involve healthy alignment.

During daily activities, and especially when dancing, notice the alignment of the ear, shoulder and hip. Work which requires many hours of standing, sitting, or leaning over is very demand-ing on the body. An orthodontist told me that his colleagues in the dental profession visit chiroprac-tors regularly because of the physical results of leaning over patients all day.

Awareness of posture must be a habit in every-day life to be able to dance with good posture and move in a healthy way.

Posture and society

Posture shows the world many things about our-selves. Our posture displays our energy level, emo-tions, and shows how we spend our time.

"Forward shoulder rotation," "rounded back," and *"Dowager's hump"* are terms used to describe slump-ing shoulders. This posture used to be associated with "mature" figures, but is now common in

younger age groups as well. Slumping shoulders have been partly attributed to the amount of time people spend doing sedentary desk-related activities. One dance teacher remarked that she can look at a person's posture and tell how much education they have, because it is apparent from the alignment of their head and shoulders how much of their time is spent sitting at a desk.

Our society has reduced its emphasis on good posture. My parents and grandparents used to emphasize proper alignment and remind their children to "sit up straight," but nowadays most people in our culture don't seem to think about it much. Rather than emphasizing correct posture, our society is manufacturing furniture and clothing that are comfortable for a rounded back. Notice the way that many modern chairs place the body into a slumped position, versus antique styles which encourage sitting up straight.

Posture with a *"rounded back"* is so common that sewing teachers give instructions on how to construct clothing for it, and ready-made clothing is designed with this posture in mind. One of my early dance teachers commented on the prolific use of shoulder pads in business suits. She speculates that this is because shoulder pads help visually compensate for rounded shoulders.

No wonder so many people in our society have neck and back problems! Some students told me that their chiropractors were amazed at how much their neck and shoulder conditions improved after taking belly dance classes.

Posture and dance technique

Most belly dance teachers emphasize correct posture because of its relationship to dance movements. An added benefit of good posture is that it helps a dancer look slender and healthy. Posture misalignments, such as slumped shoulders, locked knees, and swayed back, make it impossible to gain a full range of motion during hip, shoulder and abdominal movements.

If the knees are "locked" (totally straight), it creates a chain reaction throughout the body, restricting range of movement all over. Belly dance teachers remind students to *"bend your knees!"* Other common refrains are *"lift your chest,"* and *"lengthen your lower back,"* all reminders of postural alignment.

I found it amusing when a beginner-level student described a belly dance class as *"a posture class taken to the extreme."* Students sometimes don't see the reason for this emphasis. Slightly bending the knees allows the lower spine to lengthen. This allows for larger abdominal movements, such as belly rolls, flutters, and undulations. Erect shoulders permit greater range of motion in upper body movements such as rib cage lifts, drops, shoulder shimmies and all other related movements.

If you are having problems developing good posture, classes in Alexander Technique, Feldenkreis Technique, and yoga are good resources, in addition to a dance instructor with expertise.

Posture and emotion

Apart from dance technique issues, posture shows various *feelings*. For example, in everyday speech the term "nervous energy" describes a specific behavior, and the posture of a person with nervous energy is different from the posture of a lethargic person. There are many other types of energy which are shown by posture. For example, slumped shoulders may give the impression that the dancer is tired, or we may interpret it as a sign of depression, back problems, or lack of training.

Dancers generally want to convey an uplifted feeling of joy and project an image of beauty, and good posture helps project that. Speech coaches train politicians and actors to place their weight on the balls of the feet in "ready to speak" position when greeting an audience. This projects a friendlier feeling than weight placement on the heels. After the greeting, the weight is evenly distributed on the feet, with posture in alignment in a neutral stance.

Gentle, nurturing, outwardly projected energy, such as between a parent and a child, is expressed by the parent's posture leaning toward the child, directing loving energy toward them. Similarly, leaning forward toward the audience while onstage, with outstretched arms in a "giving" pose or other projection of positive energy, shows friendly, outgoing feelings. The giving pose directed to the side or into space creates a more general impression of positive energy flowing outward into the world, rather than directed toward specific people (see photo on page 29).

Posture is a nonverbal form of communication, and may be used in a more obvious manner. A psychology professor told her class to ask someone for a favor, and then to watch their body language. If they said "yes," but pulled away with their body, then the real answer was "no," and they had no intent of fulfilling the promise. American modern dance pioneer Martha Graham reminded dancers that *"movement never lies."*[7]

In dance, movements which are in opposition or conflicting with one another can convey two halves of an abstract design, opposites, mixed feelings, or chaos, depending on the feeling that the dancer chooses to express. For example, a dancer waving to the audience in a friendly way while leaning away from them is conveying a mixed message.

The intent of the dancer, her facial expression and other nuances flavor the message she sends to the audience. She could be using conflicting gestures with awareness as part of an abstract design or comedy routine, or she could be reacting to an audience by subconsciously pulling away from them.

Breath as energy

Breathing is one of the most basic ways of drawing energy into the body. The breath has rhythms:

• Continuously flowing in and out, *or*
• Inspiration, pausing (suspension of the breath) and exhalation.

While a dancer's breathing is not immediately apparent to the audience, the rhythm of the breath is shown on a subliminal level through the movements she is performing. For example, a slow, evenly flowing undulation or camel movement requires that the rhythm of the breath flow with the rhythm of the movement.

Holding a breath (suspended breathing) is a reaction to feelings of suspense and anticipation. Sometimes, too, we hold our breath due to stress while trying to perform a movement which is challenging for us. The rest of the body may join the suspense and freeze too, and the audience may sense this. Some dance movements require controlled, suspended breathing; the diaphragm flutter is performed using a held breath.

Inhaling a deep breath is associated with making a great effort, or with feeling a strong emotion, or with trying to control our emotions. During a deep inhalation, the abdomen flexes forward. In belly dance, we take a deep breath during certain abdominal movements, such as very large, slow undulations and belly rolls.

Irregular breathing (an uneven pattern of inhalation and exhalation) is associated with fear and feeling agitated. Shallow, quick breathing, panting or "catching" our breath after intense effort or physical exercise shows our level of exertion. During shallow breathing, the chest and shoulders rise, resulting in less oxygen intake than deep abdominal breathing. We may also interpret shallow breathing as a sign of suffering, depending on the posture and mannerisms that accompany the breath.

Being aware of the patterns of breathing helps dancers relax and move efficiently. Awareness of breathing patterns and use of deep breathing is also an integral part of yoga practices. Because of this, yoga classes are especially helpful for devel-

Aquilah in an artistic pose. The outstretched arms and hands express feminine energy flowing outward.

oping awareness of breathing patterns, and coordinating them with physical movement.

Exercises:

Posture check: Have someone take a photo of you from the side, standing in a neutral, relaxed position. Evaluate your alignment. Are your ear, shoulder and hip aligned? Do you feel the weight evenly distributed on the soles of both feet?

Posture during dance movements: Sense and observe how your posture changes during dance move-

ments. If you place your hands on your lower back, you will feel the changes in the alignment of your spine during lower body movements. Standing sideways to a mirror is also helpful. Experiment with your favorite steps or with these movements:

- Undulations/camels
- Step-together-step touch
- Chest lift and drop
- Pushing navel outward
- Pulling navel inward

Posture habits: Check your posture periodically throughout the day, aligning the ear, shoulder and hip. How does good posture feel to you? How does bad posture feel? Notice the sensations in your body when you are in alignment versus out of alignment. What are your challenges with maintaining good posture during your daily activities?

Breathing: Practice simple movements, observing your natural flow of breath as you practice. Use these movements, or other steps of your choice:

• Stride four steps sideways, then forward four steps *(vary tempo from slow to fast)*
• Lift and lower arms *(varying tempo of arms)*

After observing the way your breath naturally accompanies these movements, experiment with other common dance movements, and notice the manner in which your breath naturally flows. This exercise helps develop awareness of breathing patterns while dancing.

CHAPTER THREE

Energy and Creative Expression

"You must have chaos within you to give birth to a dancing star."

FRIEDRICH NIETZSCHE (1844–1900), GERMAN PHILOSOPHER

*P*utting energy into movements seems like it would be a simple subject, but it isn't. There are many levels of energy between *"give it all you've got"* and *"I'm so tired I can barely move."* Varying levels of energy evoke different feelings. Projecting energy outward to the audience demands skill and creative interpretation by the dancer.

Creating and expressing energy

In this section, we'll discuss ways of creating and expressing energy using the following characteristics:

- *Tempo*
- *Imagery*
- *Buildup and decrease in force*
- *Level*
- *Sustained flow*
- *Percussive*
- *Shaking*
- *Swinging*
- *Suspended*
- *Collapse*

This list is incomplete, since there are countless ways to create and express energy!

Tempo

Slow, medium and fast movements convey different energy levels. Generally, slow movements convey leisurely, relaxed, deliberate, meditative or introspective feelings. Medium tempos convey outgoing, friendly, fun, "let me entertain you" feelings. Fast tempo movements (such as hip shimmies) convey feelings of heightened excitement, abundant energy, or urgency. Tempo changes within the dances you create enhance communication with your audience, interaction with your music, and convey feelings and a particular mood.

Imagery

Dance is a physical form of expressing feelings, abstract ideas and images. Using images is an effective way to show energy level. For example, the way a dancer handles a veil can project many different energy levels. The dancer may hold the veil like a baby, touch it gently like a piece of fine fabric, or handle it roughly like a piece of cheap fabric. Each of these calls for a different level of energy projected outward into the veil.

In one of Ibrahim Farrah's seminars, he told students to move like birds during an arm movement; to imagine that the arms were wings.[8] This resulted in a soft, flowing energy level. During another movement, he told us to imagine "creeping like a cat" which created a slow, sustained energy level.

Building up and decreasing in force

I remember Ibrahim Farrah telling a student during a workshop to decrease the amount of energy she was putting into a movement. He said, *"you're giving it too much."* He advised putting more energy into the movement as the music was increasing in power, and waiting to *"give it all you've got"* when the music neared its climactic point.[9] Varying levels of intensity in music call for varying levels of intensity in dance movements.

Ibrahim Farrah was a master of varying energy levels, particularly by using sequential movements and gradually increasing their power. He used sequential movements to build up the energy level in a dance to correspond with the emphasis of the music. Experiment with how this idea may be useful in your own dances. For example, a small hip

shimmy gradually increasing in size to your biggest hip shimmy, or a small arm movement evolving into a bigger arm movement.

Musically, increasing and decreasing force is heard in the qualities of contrasting loud sounds with soft sounds, and fast sounds with slow sounds during a song. Similarly, professional public speakers and actors are told to use "voice variety" (loud, soft, fast and slow phrases) to keep audiences interested in what they're saying.

Dance variety, like voice variety, is essential to good performances. A dancer who uses the same rate of speed and the same amount of energy throughout a dance is like a speaker talking in a monotone. Like a monotone speaker, a monotone dancer causes the audience to lose interest. In contrast, a dancer who uses variety is interesting to watch and is probably enjoying herself more, because using variety is fun.

An example of increasing force would be gradually to raise the arms as the music builds up in force. Along with this, a corresponding hip movement also increases in size, going from a small hip movement to a big, bold movement. Decreasing force could be shown by using big, strong arm movements which gradually become softer and smaller as the music changes.

Level

Level (height) changes express many feelings. Level is manipulated by bending or straightening the knees, going up on tiptoe, raising and lowering the arms, or by using floorwork.[10]

An uplifted body and upward gestures convey a feeling of loftiness, spirituality, joy, prayer, lightness or bliss. Being on the floor is traditionally associated with going into a state of meditation, trance, pain, pleasure, intense emotion, prayer and the primal nature of life.

OPPOSITE: *Ramona dancing at floor level, rising from a backbend.*

Standing up after being seated or rising from a floor pose is associated with taking control and with being strong. (Politicians and other public speakers stand up when giving a speech in order to take control of a meeting or press conference, and to hold their audience's attention.)

The way we interpret a level change depends on the dancer's posture, facial expressions, gestures and movements that accompany the body level.

Sustained flow

Sustained, flowing energy maintains one level of effort and stays there. All the belly dance songs I've ever heard contain sections which sound like they're "flowing." Songs using string instruments or synthesized music tend to have longer flowing sections. If you listen carefully, you may recognize flowing, sustained energy sections within drum solos as well. Dance movements which continuously flow, such as smooth repeating traveling steps, smooth arm movements or smooth hip movements go along with "flowing" music.

Percussive energy

Drumbeats are the heartbeats of belly dance music. A dancer must understand rhythm in order

Elegance and flowing energy projected with veils during a performance by Xtine, director of Mangelly Danz Club (Augusta, Georgia).

to dance well. It is critical that dancers know the basic rhythms in belly dance music. In addition, staccato-like accents can also come from the flute or other unexpected sources.

Dancers often interpret percussive accents in music with sharp, isolated body movements, generally using hip, rib or shoulder movements. However, many other options are available. Experiment with staccato-like accents using arms, head movements, and directional changes. The possibilities are limitless.

Shaking energy

Shimmies and *vibrations* are not restricted to the hips and shoulders. Hand vibrations, leg "freezes," diaphragm flutters and other vibrating and shaking movements reflect the vibrating sounds so characteristic in Oriental belly dance music. The hip shimmy, in particular, is a favorite audience-pleaser. It's exciting to watch, and it expresses passion.

Be aware of your use of floor space while doing vibrational and shimmy movements. Some dancers have a tendency to "plant" themselves in one spot on the stage during the shimmy portion of a dance. Speaking coaches advise, *"don't be like a tree, because it's more interesting to watch someone move around."* However, dancers may choose to dance in place, and this can also be extremely effective.[11]

Swinging energy

Swinging movements trace an arc. Possibilities include a half moon shape traced with a toe, hips, arms, head, shoulders or veil. These tracings can be rotated in many directions, and are often exciting highlights of a belly dance performance. Swinging motions convey the feeling of energy release and freedom of movement.

Zar, trance and meditation dances also contain swinging or swaying motions, particularly with the upper body and hair.[12] These dances tradition-ally served as a way to release stress and relieve depression. *Khaliji* (Gulf) dances also feature swinging motions of the hair.

The possibilities for including swinging motions in your dances are limitless, and your choice reflects your interpretation of the music.

Suspended energy

One of the first choreography tips I received was that *"stopping all movement for a few seconds is a good dramatic accent."* Select a step you like, then suspend the movement by pausing, holding it for a second. This provides an effective, contrasting accent to traveling steps or high-energy movements. Dancers may stop movements in midair; they seem momentarily *suspended*. For example, an arabesque pose with one leg extended in the air behind the dancer creates a graceful picture.

Professional speakers sometimes pause for a few seconds (they silently count *"one, two, three"*) and then resume talking. An Atlanta speech coach calls this a "refreshing" pause, because it grabs the audience's attention and makes the words which were just spoken stand out. It gives the audience a moment to absorb the content of the speech thus far. Pauses during a dance serve in much the same way; the pause gives the audience an opportunity to absorb the visual image of the dancer's prior movements.

Have you seen dancers who never seemed to pause? If you have, it's likely that you don't remember much about their performance other than the fact that the dancer never seemed to stop until the music ended. Here is why:

A fundamental truth in drumming is that one way to accent a note is to have a pause following it. The pause after the beat makes it stand apart from the other notes which have been strung together. This also applies to dance; a pose which the dancer holds for a few seconds stands out from strings of movements which are linked.

Here is a visual example:

xxxxxxxxxxxxxxx x xxxxxxxxxxxxxxx

The center "x" in the above example stands out from the others, because it is not linked with them.

The dance pose or drumbeat which stands apart does not necessarily have any more effort or difficulty to it; simply the fact that it stands alone calls our attention to it and makes it memorable.

Collapsing energy

Collapsing energy is directed downward. Just as a song's intensity may build to a peak, there is sometimes a sudden, contrasting reduction in force in the music. Some options for showing collapsing movements include use of kneeling positions, bent-knee positions or arm movements directed downward.

Many other ideas for dramatic expression are available. I've integrated collapsing energy into beginner dances by using poses with the eyes focused on the floor, and suddenly dropping the arms from an overhead position to hip level. For example, I choreographed a dance using downward flowing finger ripples to interpret a rapidly decreasing musical energy level in a song.

Belly dancers who are athletically inclined may use dramatic changes in body level to show collapsing energy. The classic example of this is a sudden drop from a standing sustained spin into a complete backbend on the floor. It is necessary to be flexible, strong, and to get professional coaching to learn this movement.[13]

Remember that collapsing energy does not have to be physically demanding to be effective. A finger ripple may be as good as a backbend for showing a collapsing sound in the music. Tailor your dance to what feels most comfortable for *you*, and fits your own physical condition and personal artistic preferences.

Variety and personal interpretation

All these things we've been discussing are based on an individual's preferences and unique interpretation of music. Your decision to interpret a segment of music as percussive may not correspond with another dancer's interpretation. I've interpreted flute music with percussive, angular dance movements, which is not the way many of my colleagues would interpret it.

Each dancer is an individual and this shows in your dances. Energy level is your personal expression of emotion. One of the secrets of creating fabulous dances is to include *all* these varying energy levels in your dances. Great music also contains varying energy levels (loud, soft, fast and slow tempos and pauses).

When we talk about energy level, we're getting to the core of being an artist. Energy is something so individual that it cannot be replicated. Dancers performing identical step patterns do not have the same emotional expression due to their variations in energy.

Slight variations of identical movements among troupe members show individual personalities. Subtle variations of physical characteristics including hand position, facial expression, and shoulder position are just a few indications. Each of us is a unique individual with unique feelings, and our responses to music are personal. What sounds percussive to you, may sound "flowing" to someone else.

Interpreting and reflecting on how music makes you *feel,* and then outwardly showing your interpretation makes you a unique artist whose work cannot be duplicated. There is not one "correct" interpretation of music. Music that sounds like a hip shimmy to you may sound to someone else like a flowing arm movement. This is where technique ends and individual artistry begins.

OPPOSITE: *Aspyn tracing an arc with her veil.*

Exercises:

Imagery: Select an image from nature. (Examples: fish, cat, camel, windblown leaf, butterfly, ocean wave.) Dance how your selected image would travel across the room. (Example: to echo a windblown leaf, you might use a meandering floor pattern of steps.) Dance the image several times, varying your speed of travel: *slow, medium, fast.* Then repeat your steps again, this time adding occasional pauses between steps.

Build up in force/decrease in force: Select a step, movement, or combination of movements that you already know (examples: crossover steps, hip circles, snake arms). Dance the movement with the following qualities:

- Begin with small steps, gradually increasing to big steps.
- Begin with big, bold hip movements, gradually making them smaller.
- Begin with big arm movements, gradually making them softer.

Level changes: What body level do you usually use? Experiment with adding variety to dance combinations you already know by changing levels. Examples include doing movements in *relevé* (high on balls of feet or tiptoe), *plié* (bent knees), and floor positions. Add even more variety by doing steps and movements with one foot flat and one in *relevé*.

Sustained flow: Select a traveling step you already know, and a piece of music you feel comfortable with. Make your traveling steps smooth, visualizing the steps as a flowing stream or river. Dance the step with the following qualities:

- Slow steps
- Quick steps
- Big steps

- Little steps
- Pauses between steps

Percussive energy: Select a movement which "pops," that is, a sudden accent. (Examples: shoulder, belly and hip accents). Using a percussive song or drum solo, improvise a dance using pops to articulate accents in the song. Use flowing movements between accents to connect them. Include the following qualities in your improvisation:

- Big movements
- Little movements
- Alternating movements
- Pauses between movements

Shaking and vibrations: Start with a basic shimmy (examples: shoulder shimmy, hip shimmy). Now, transfer the vibrating quality to different parts of the body (examples: hand tremors, knees, belly, head, foot). Discover how you can vary a basic shimmy by transferring the motion to different parts of the body and by varying the tempo (fast, medium, slow).

Swinging: Imagine something that swings. (Examples: a child's swing at the playground, a pendulum, a leaf blowing in the wind, an orchestra's conductor waving his baton). Visualizing this motion, imitate it with various parts of the body. Experiment with:

- One foot
- Shoulders
- Hips
- Arms

Suspended and pausing movement: Select any movement. Now, begin the movement, but pause in the middle. For example, begin to take a step, but pause the foot (hold the position for a count or two) before completing the step. Experiment with:

- One foot
- Elbows
- Hips
- Wrists

Collapse: Emphasize a downward movement. Start with a familiar movement. (Examples: hip drop, downward shoulder movement, lowering arms from overhead position.) Visualization may help. (Examples of visual images: raindrops, a leaf slowly dropping to the ground, a silk veil gently floating to the floor.) Emphasize your selected downward movement by:

- Varying the size of the selected downward movement from small to big.
- Transferring the downward movement from one part of the body to another (example: hip drop, then shoulder drop).
- Varying speed of downward movement (starting with super-slow, feeling all the nuances of the movement).

Variety: Select a movement or combination of movements that you already know. Dance the selected movement or combination several times, each time using a different quality:

- Percussive (emphasize accents)
- Shaking (shimmy or vibration)
- Floating (soft, light, effortless movements)
- Bouncing (up and down movements)
- Smooth (connected movements that flow in a pattern)
- Slow
- Fast

Small vs. big: Notice that movements involving smaller body parts (fingers, elbows, wrists, knees) evoke different energy levels than movements involving bigger body parts (shoulders, arms, legs, torso, hips). Dance the following patterns, alternating between small and big body parts of your choice, noticing which create more delicate movements and which are more forceful:

- Circle
- Diamond
- Figure 8
- Star
- Spell your initials

CHAPTER FOUR

Music, Style and Individuality

*"The face is the mirror of the mind, and the
eyes without speaking confess the secrets of the heart."*

SAINT JEROME (374–419 A.D.)

*B*elly dancers wear many different kinds of costumes to highlight their personal style and individuality. Whether you wear a beaded *bedlah* (cabaret costume), folkloric costume, tassels and cotton skirts, dance pants and fringe, or a fusion of costume styles, you must select music and decide how you will fuse that music with your dance.

Oriental dance emphasizes internal muscular control (*isolations*, particularly of the torso, hips, chest, head, arms and hands), while many other forms of dance emphasize traveling steps or footwork. The unique flavors of belly dance music call for different styles of dancing. The dancer/choreographer must select an approach to using the music to fuse with the dance. Individual preferences are expressed in:

- *Mirroring the music*
- *Counting beats*
- *Contrasting the music*
- *Personality*
- *Facial expression*
- *Eye contact*
- *Stage makeup*
- *Gestures*

Mirroring the music

The Near Eastern style of belly dancing traditionally involves the dancer mirroring the dynamics of the music. This idea is used extensively in most forms of dance. Jazz dancers call this *"movement that goes bop when the music goes bop,"* or movement that mirrors the same dynamics as the music.

OPPOSITE: *Gestures of the arms and hands express energy, style, and emotion. (Photo of Coco courtesy of the artist.)*

Example:

- Music is fast, and the dancer moves fast.
- Music is slow, and the dancer moves slowly.
- Music pauses, and the dancer pauses.

This is an effective and traditional approach. In belly dance and most other dance forms, movements that reflect the music exactly are very effective, and it's good to stay with the music most of the time. However, too much mirroring causes dances to be too predictable, without spontaneity.

For example, have you seen a group or soloist dancing *so* much with the beat of the music that you sense them silently counting, "1, 2, 3, . . . ," and then see them thinking *"we've gone to the right, now we need to go left"*? This overuse of counting and mirroring exact accents may result in a dance that is too predictable.

Some dancers call this dancing *with* the music, or dancing *on top of* the music, instead of dancing *in* the music. The most emotionally expressive and compelling belly dancers are those who dance *in* the music. *Entrainment* refers to "being *in* the music," and comes from a deep understanding of the music, while being relaxed and focused.

Counting beats

The relationship between dancing and counting beats can be a love/hate relationship. On one hand, counting beats is extremely useful for students, particularly at the beginner and intermediate levels, and helps the instructor in getting their ideas across with clarity. Counting beats keeps duets and troupes in sync. However, dancers and instructors can become too dependent on counting beats, leaving no room for spontaneity.

Part of the soulful expression of belly dance is its apparent spontaneity, and this needs to be balanced with the need to count beats. It's a balancing act easier said than done. One of the things that makes a great dancer is her passion, which

is shown, in part, by her spontaneity. Having occasional contrasting, unexpected elements in a dance give it a spur-of-the-moment feeling and appearance.

Contrasting the music

Occasional use of contrast is very effective. In music, two instruments contrasting each other rhythmically is called *counterpoint*. In dance, the mixture of complimentary movements with contrasting movements is interesting and artistically pleasing.

Examples of effective use of contrast in Oriental dance:

- *A dancer in Egypt:* during a segment of the drum solo, the intensity of the drums increased to a very high level, with a rapidly pulsating beat. Rather than reflecting the driving force of the music, she contrasted the pulsating drumbeats with a very slow, lingering shoulder circle. This was a memorable highlight in her dance. After this highlight, she returned to movements which exactly reflected the accents of the music.
- *A dancer in Lebanon:* her contract required wearing very high heels for her performances. At one point during her carefully planned choreography, she became so uncomfortable with the shoes that she spontaneously and forcefully kicked them off. The audience loved her spontaneity; they said, "she's so *passionate!*" There was such a positive response from the audience that they told her to keep the shoe-kicking as part of the choreography.

Using contrasting movements with the music is an advanced technique, and is like using a strong spice; a little goes a long way. A dash of pepper is good, but too much ruins the recipe. Using contrast is an outward showing of your personal interpretation of the music and how it makes you feel. It's part of your self-expression, your soul, and beyond imitation. Dancing spontaneously captures and expresses the feeling of joy in movement.

Your personality, your dance

Years ago, students asked an Atlanta instructor to teach them how to put personality into their dances. The class specifically asked to learn her trademark gestures. This instructor has a flirtatious, cute style which suits her. However, her style will not fit all students. A dancer whose personality is more reserved than extroverted will not feel comfortable flirting with an audience.

Showing your own personality is better than being a copy of someone else. Dance is really all about emotion, and what audiences truly want to see is the dancer's unique personality and soul expressed in movement. If you're not an extrovert, don't feel that you have to act that way to be a great dancer. The dance masters of the world come with all kinds of personalities, and each express themselves in ways that suit them individually.

Solid technique is important, but the most emotionally powerful dancer I've seen did not perform the most complex, intricate movements. The physical expression and the dancer's raw emotional power was intense, and the movements, though technically good, were not the focus of the dance.

This is the true essence of dance: dancing coming from within the *soul*, entrained in the *music*, speaking with the *body*.

Facial expression and focal points

Researcher Paul Eckman found that the human face is capable of more than 10,000 expressions.[14] Facial expression is one of the most basic ways of displaying emotion, and is important during all phases of a dance. Having awareness of facial expressions is especially important when exerting effort, because expressions can become strained during intense exercise or dance movements. We can become more aware of our facial expressions with practice.

Your eyes accent and highlight your movements. Audiences look in the direction the performer looks. For example, if you look down at your hip during a hip movement, the audience will also look at your hip.

Be aware that focusing in different areas changes your facial expression. When focusing on something at a distance, your eyes will open wider than when focusing on something nearby. Like traveling steps in dances, eyes should also move around and not stare in one spot. Staring at the audience too long makes them feel uneasy.

Having variety in focal points is important. I have seen troupes which focused outward toward the audience during their entire dance, while their hips and shoulders were doing beautiful movements. This disconnection between the head and the body sends the disconcerting message that the intellect/mind is separate from the body. The loveliness of belly dance is that it includes the entire body, and is not a dance from the neck down.

Changing focus points makes dances more interesting, and increases feeling and emotional involvement. Focus point examples:

- Up
- Down
- Near
- Far
- Back
- Side
- Eye contact

Eye contact expertise

Making eye contact with different areas of an audience while on the stage is like having nonverbal "conversations." Some dancers choose not to

Eye contact with the audience during a performance makes the dance conversational.
(Oracle's photo courtesy of Dance of the Fates.)

make eye contact with the audience. I've seen enthralling dancers who go into a trance-like state when performing, and are focusing on their own inner world. This can be very beautiful. On the other hand, the audience may see it as cold or lacking in feeling. The interpretation depends on the setting of the dance, the intent and skill level of the dancer, and the mood of the audience.

For example, a dancer performing for a small group at a home birthday party is expected to interact with the audience with eye contact, conversation with the guests, and focusing her attention on the person celebrating a birthday. In contrast, a dancer performing on a large stage is separated from the audience and is expected to have less direct interaction with them.

Flowing segments of the dance are good opportunities to establish eye contact with the audience. Remember that dance is a communication skill, similar to talking. Eye contact keeps the audience involved and interested by making the dance "conversational." Suggestions for eye contact include having random "conversations" in different areas of the audience.

While on the stage under strong lights, you may not see individuals in the audience. This is because most theaters are set up for the audience to be in semi-darkness while the stage is set up with strong lights on the performers. Under these circumstances, the performer gives the illusion of seeing members of the audience when looking toward them, although, in reality, she cannot see them individually.

Stage makeup

Makeup application and false eyelashes are important on the stage and in photography, to help features show well from a distance and under strong lights. Emotions and feelings are shown in part by facial expressions, and makeup helps define facial features so that facial expressions are visible to the audience from a distance. Stage makeup colors and application techniques are different from everyday makeup, since stage makeup must help the performer "project" her personality and style from a distance.

If you need help with makeup application, there are helpful instructional resources available at libraries, bookstores and by mail-order (see Resources). Some salons offer makeup application lessons with a professional makeup artist.

Another option for getting help with stage makeup is to consult with a professional performer or teacher in your area. Look for someone who wears well-applied stage makeup. Department store cosmetics departments may (or may not) be helpful.

Gestures

Gestures are *specific* or *nonspecific*, and simple or complex designs. Whereas some specific facial expressions have the same meaning across cultures[15], meanings of many specific gestures are defined within cultures.

Dance of the Fates tribal fusion troupe. From left: Fatina, Liora, Oracle.

Gestures clarify the meaning of spoken words. Habitual gestures also sometimes find their way into dances. (Photos of Ramona.)

Specific gestures are like words drawn with the body; the audience instantly understands them. Examples: waving *"hello,"* pointing to indicate a direction *("up, down, over there"),* or palms together "praying hands." Other gestures are abstract designs which are nonspecific; for example, a flourish or twirl of the hand has different meanings, depending on the context of what is said along with the hand movement.

A dancer clapping her hands on the stage is asking the audience, nonverbally, to clap in time with the music, and so they begin keeping time by clapping. At the end of the dance, the audience applauds the dancer because she's signaled that the dance is over and the time has come to applaud. She takes a bow (another gesture) to graciously accept their applause and say "thank-you" nonverbally. These are all examples of *specific gestures.*

Some specific gestures are universal, while others have meanings which vary from culture to culture. For example, the "OK" sign of the connected thumb and forefinger in American culture means something entirely different in other cultures; meanings vary from "coin," "worthless," "zero," and even to obscenity in various areas of the world. Thus, it is important to know the meaning of specific gestures when dancing for ethnic audiences.

Nonspecific gestures are abstract. A wide, sweeping movement of the hands may convey the flowing feeling of a certain part of a piece of music, or suggest the contours of a landscape. Just as in conversation we "speak" with our hands sometimes, it is the same with dance. Nonspecific abstract designs of the hands and body express ideas and feelings which cannot be expressed with words.

Finally, some nonspecific gestures are uniquely individual. One of my dance teachers uses a unique hand gesture to tell her musicians to speed up the tempo; I've never seen another dancer use that gesture. Just as each of us has a preferred way of using our hands in daily conversations, the same is true of dance.

Simple gestures have the power to move us deeply. For example:

A dancer was performing at the golden wedding anniversary party of an elderly couple; the wife was seated at a banquet table, while the dancer was performing. Guests were enjoying themselves, watching the dancer, swaying and clapping with the music. The elderly woman put her hands on the table in front of her, and with great effort, slowly pushed herself up into a standing position, supporting herself with the table in front of her. With obvious effort, she made small hip-lifting dance movements. This simple gesture brought tears to the eyes of the guests; the elderly woman was making a profound nonverbal statement with the simple gesture of standing up and moving her hips, because it took great effort for her.

Complex gestures create beautiful geometric and abstract designs, like motifs and colors in an Oriental carpet. They can create a beautiful picture, or the audience may read them as "busy," depending on the skill and intent of the dancer.

Hands that are "busy" or "twitchy," that is, moving in small, quick, repetitive abstract gestures, may "read" to the audience as "she is nervous." Hands which are too busy distract the audience, like a speaker who uses her hands too much and causes the audience to focus on the hands, rather than on her words.

Many beautiful and mesmerizing dances have been performed using only gestures and design motifs drawn with the hands. To do this effectively, the dancer needs to move with awareness, using the arms and hands to illustrate designs, rather than having the hands going through motions without awareness.

Graceful arms and hands

The hands and arms are among the most expressive tools of the dancer. They have a language of their own and express joy, sorrow, and the whole gamut of emotions. Arms and hands are the messengers of the heart.

One of the most commonly asked questions in dance class is *"what do I do with my arms during this (fill in the blank) movement?"*

The answer is that the hand and arm position, whatever it is (for example, arms in an L position), needs to be *definite*. When the arms and hands are held in a controlled manner, they convey energy and powerful presence. When the arms and hands droop, they convey wimpy and weak energy. A hand and arm may be straight, or may look "soft" with a bent elbow and wrist, but both of these styles convey feminine energy as long as the arms and hands are positioned with awareness.

Be particularly aware of the position of your hands and elbows; proper positioning makes your poses and gestures beautiful, and projects strength and vitality. Practicing in front of a mirror is helpful.

Exercises:

Adding contrast: Select a piece of music to which you usually do a specific movement. For example, select a piece of music that you use for hip or shoulder shimmies. Next, select a contrasting movement to use with this music, instead of using the shimmy. Experiment with using fingertips, elbows, feet or head to interpret this music. Try big, small, fast and slow movements.

Focal points: Dance to any song of your choice, varying focal points: up, down, sideways, front, back.

Gesture: Select a gesture. (Examples: finger snaps, clapping, wave "hello" or "goodbye," nod head "yes," shake head "no.") How would you put this movement into a dance?

Role model gestures: Consider adapting a gesture from your favorite role model to suit your own personality and performance. What nonspecific gestures, steps and body movements could you adapt for use in your own dances?

Gesture habits: Do you have "trademark" movements or habitual gestures? Watch a recording of yourself or recall past performances. Do you see a specific feeling or trait you frequently express?

Moving pictures combination:

- Find a few poses (four or five) from this book or other sources. Look for poses in belly dance magazines, websites, or advertising. Sketch them or print them out.
- Lay the pictures out and arrange them in an order; select one as a beginning pose, then

select an ending pose, and put the rest in the middle in an order which pleases you.
- Connect the poses with movement. Dance your way from your beginning pose through your ending pose.

Evaluate the dance phrase (combination) you created. How does it look, how does it feel? Could you create a whole dance based on variations of this combination? To create variations, experiment with varying the tempo (fast, medium, slow), and adding pauses.

Mastering complex techniques: Select a step or movement which is challenging for you. Think about the movement, and what it looks like when you've seen it performed just right. Does it remind you of something? For example, the "camel" movement reminds us of a camel. Next, perform the movement while visualizing the image you found. (Example: visualize an ocean wave to simplify an undulation or belly roll.)

Visualization is a powerful tool for mastering new movements. I used the visual image of a fish to master certain abdominal movements. Many movements in belly dance come from movements found in nature: camel/camel step; snakes/snake arms; inchworm/crawling floor movement.

Some dancers enjoy using geometric shapes as a basis for building movements. Experiment with using both animal movement patterns and geometric images to find out which are most helpful for you.

Integrated isolations: Another powerful tool for mastering dance movements is understanding *isolations* and *integration*. *Isolations* are movements which appear to be confined to one part of the body, while the rest of the body appears motionless.

OPPOSITE: *Coco demonstrates the power of hands and arms to express feminine strength and vitality. (Photo courtesy of the artist.)*

(Example: in a shoulder shimmy, the shoulders move rapidly forwards and backwards while the rest of the body appears still.)

Despite the appearance that one part of the body is moving alone, movements require different parts of our bodies to work together. Thus, the body is a complex *integrated* system of muscles, bones, connective tissue, etc., all working together. Experiment with basic isolations, noticing sensations in nonmoving body parts:

- Hip slide and circle (sense the weight shifts on the soles of the feet).
- Head slide (notice sensations in shoulders and back).
- Finger ripple or play finger cymbals (notice muscle movements in forearms).
- Hip shimmy (notice sensations in lower abdomen and lower back).

Understanding integration is particularly important in mastering complex isolations, because many parts of the body must work together to produce the desired effect. For example, the diaphragm flutter is an advanced isolation in which the diaphragm goes rapidly up and down, creating the visual effect of an upper belly flutter.

However, far from being a movement which exercises only the upper belly, the flutter requires a specific breathing technique, and exercises muscles in the neck, rib cage, spine and more. Although this movement appears isolated, it is a movement of many parts of the body working together.

Visualizing the movement as a laugh without sound or "inner jogging" helps to simplify the flutter. Coaching from a qualified instructor is often needed in order to learn this complex movement.[16] What other movements do you know which appear isolated, but are actually integrated?

Knowledge based on appearance: We subconsciously absorb a wealth of information from the appearance of another person. A fiction writing teacher showed her class a photo of a woman, then asked them to write a biography of what they thought her life may have been like. The teacher was astonished when the written bios accurately reflected many factors of the woman's life. The subject photo she showed was a close relative of whom she knew many details including the era when the photo was taken, the woman's age, eating habits, and personality.

Look closely at any photo of a person in a magazine or newspaper, particularly noticing her/his facial expression, makeup, gestures, and anything else that gives you clues about personality. What do you know or sense about the subject? This exercise helps us be aware that we are absorbing intuitive information every day. On stage, when people see us dance they absorb a variety of information about us. It is important for a performer to be aware of what their expressions, makeup, gestures, costume and movements are "saying" nonverbally.

PART II:

DESIGNING A DANCE

CHAPTER FIVE

Artistic Design Concepts

"Spontaneity is genius in dramatic interpretation. Predetermination of expression is art. Perfection is the harmonious blending of the two."

FRANÇOIS DELSARTE (1811–1871), ON THE SCIENCE OF APPLIED AESTHETICS

A dance, whether choreographed or improvisational, includes a diversity of artistic design elements. Staged dances are essentially a series of moving pictures; that is, poses and movements put to music and performed for an audience. Concepts from other visual arts also apply to dance.

Master choreographer Ibrahim Farrah once compared the woven designs in Oriental carpets to designs in Oriental dance.[17] Oriental carpet designs include a diversity of shapes, colors and contrasts, which are linked together into a unified design. These carpets also have repeating motifs which express a characteristic Oriental style. In this chapter, we'll discuss the elements that bring a dance together into a unified design. (Chapters 13-14 discuss the way that several of these ideas apply to music.)

Floor patterns

Spatial patterns, also called *floor patterns*, are the pathways a dancer takes when traveling around the stage. These are like an Oriental carpet design or a map laid out on the floor, that helps dance movements flow smoothly. One of my

RIGHT:
Detail of an Oriental carpet showing design motifs.

OPPOSITE:
Ramona at sunrise on Jekyll Island. Photo by Beautiful Photos, Inc.

teachers made it a point to remind students to use the entire stage area; for the time you're on the stage, she said "it all belongs to you."

On the other hand, many effective dances have been performed standing in place or by using small floor patterns. Kalila of Atlanta performed a very memorable dance while seven months pregnant. She stood in one place and did a mesmerizing series of movements using only her hands, arms, and facial expression. It made such an impression that I heard about it for years afterward from friends who were in the audience.

Traditionally, many dance performances in the Near East took place in small cafes and living rooms, resulting in dances which involved more "on the spot" movements, and thus they minimized traveling steps. With today's large auditoriums and stages, dances have evolved into covering more stage area with traveling steps, partly because performance settings have changed.

There are no rules about floor patterns. The important thing is to be aware of the spatial patterns you are creating. Floor patterns help a dance flow.

Elements of cohesion

Songs, choreographies and improvisational dances include:

> *Themes,*
> *Motifs,*
> *Transitions* and
> *Repetitions.*

Theme

A theme is the central idea of a dance or a song. In a dance, the theme can be a general design idea or a series of specific movements upon which the rest of the dance is based.

For example, an Ancient Egyptian theme dance could include music reminiscent of the ancient world, with a stylized costume, poses and dance movements based on ancient artwork. This dance could include stylized poses which are repeated for emphasis.

Another example of a theme could be a star-shaped design. The dance could include using dance steps in a floor pattern in a star shape, use of arms or veil movements which go upward (toward the stars). Costuming could include shiny fabrics (reminiscent of twinkling stars).

A percussive theme could use sharp, precise hip and shoulder articulations (emphasizing percussive movement) with a drum solo instrumental, and any style of belly dance costuming.

Motif

A *motif* is an element that evokes the central idea of a dance. A dance movement or series of movements (combination), floor pattern, prop or other element can be a motif. A motif somehow characterizes a dance, like a repeating design in an Oriental carpet. A dance may have one or more motifs, and these help the improvised or choreographed dance flow.

Examples:

- Conceal and reveal themes: A veil *(motif)* covers the dancer's face during her entrance. The dancer unveils, then wraps herself in the veil during the latter part of the dance to evoke themes of concealing and revealing.
- Percussive theme: An articulated shoulder movement *(motif)* accompanies a specific accent in the music. The dancer repeats this articulated accent periodically throughout the piece, possibly with variations, evoking the theme of percussive body movement to accompany percussive music. Articulated hip movements and angular floor patterns in the same dance would be additional motifs.
- Historical Ottoman Empire theme: In *Set el Hosn* (a dance choreographed by Mohammed Khalil and performed in Egypt by Nagwa Fouad), the dancer entered the stage on an

elaborate conveyance carried by costumed men, and she carried a stylized fan. The stage set and props were motifs which evoked the theme.[18]

Transitions

A *transition* is a brief segment which links different sections of a dance or song. For example, a transition within an instrumental song can be a bridge between a section of wind instruments and a powerful drum solo. An accompanying transition in a dance may be a series of moderate tempo movements which transition from a flowing choreography into faster percussive movements to accompany the drum solo.

Contrasting movements are useful during transitions. For example, if the first part of the dance uses soft, flowing arm movements to accompany the wind instruments, the transition (bridge) could use articulated arm movements. This bridge would lead into percussive hip movements accompanying the drum solo which follows.

Repetition

Repetition of design elements is the key to making a dance cohesive. Repetition gives the dance unity, and helps it flow. This does not necessarily mean exact repetition. Repetition may be abstract: for example, a dancer may repeat a circular pattern with a shoulder movement or floor pattern, instead of repeating a previous hip circle. Another variation could be using a spiral shape instead of a true circle as a repetition. These similar repetitions evoke the feelings of the original design elements.

Using directional changes and varying floor patterns during repetitions of movements keeps the cohesive quality of the movements, but provides variation at the same time. Dances also need contrasting movements and poses, since too much repetition is boring.

An audience member made this comment after seeing a troupe dance: *"I liked a movement you did,*

but you didn't do it long enough for me to see it." Remember to give your audience enough time to see what you're doing by using repetition. Repetition is an important element in showing your abstract, nonverbal dance design.

Putting it all together

Many professional belly dancers begin by selecting a central theme (idea for the dance), and then build on it to create improvised and choreographed dances. To create an improvised or choreographed dance using a theme, select:

Theme, Scenario or Storyline (showing who, what, why, when, where and how).
Motif (dance movement(s), symbol, prop or other element that evokes the theme).
Music (which evokes the theme).
Costume (which evokes the theme).
Choreography or plan for improvisation (movements evoking the theme).

This approach is used extensively in many dance genres. The theme of the dance may, or may not, be obvious to the audience. What is most important is that the dance has a central idea which helps the dance flow, rather than having the appearance of disjointed movements assembled together.

The *theme* is the central idea around which the rest of the dance is built. A *motif* evokes the central idea, and may consist of a dance movement or combination of movements, floor patterns, props or other elements. Music which evokes the theme is selected either before or after the dance is created. Costume design is useful to evoke the theme in dances where the choreographer wants the theme to be apparent to the audience. The steps and movements in the dance evoke the theme, for example:

A professional troupe dance used an image *(theme)* of dancers riding along a conveyor belt. Steps in the dance included gliding foot-work and undulations *(motifs)*, which gave the appearance of a slow, smooth ripple. To the audience, this dance looks beautiful and well organized, and the conveyor belt image is not apparent. The reason I know about the conveyor belt image is because the choreographer told me. The audience appreciated this dance for its organization and lovely movements, and it was not necessary for them to know the theme of the dance.

In fact, some choreographers have the opinion that *not* knowing the central idea is better for the audience. This is because individual viewers who see the dance can interpret it in a way which is personal and meaningful for them as individuals.

For example, after a concert performance, a woman told me that my dance reminded her of a doll she had in her childhood. This was not the image I used on stage, but she interpreted my dance in a way that was meaningful and enjoyable for her.

Another example is a dance built around the theme song "I Put a Spell on You." The central idea of this dance was obvious, because the troupe who performed it used gestures to act out the lyrics.

Both the conveyor-belt dance and the spell-casting dances were choreographed. However, I've also seen the spell-casting dance performed as a solo, and I have no doubt that the conveyor-belt dance would also be a successful solo performance piece. Both would also work as improvisational ideas for groups or soloists.

Additional examples

Example 1: Dancing with finger cymbals is challenging for many beginner and intermediate students. I had the idea that imagining the cymbals as wind chimes effortlessly blowing in the wind would be a useful theme for building a troupe dance. (The Appendix details this dance in both a beat analysis and a chart). I hoped that using a visual image of effortlessness would make playing cymbals seem easier:

Theme: Wind chimes are ringing in the breeze.
Motif: Sound of finger cymbals to echo the theme.
Music: American belly dance instrumental.
Costume to fit theme: Any style of belly dance costuming.
Choreography: Playing a variety of rhythmic patterns with cymbals, I created a plan for using loud, soft, fast and slow sounds and tempos, coordinating with the recorded music, and using pauses/breaks in cymbal patterns. (These echo the theme of wind chimes: strong winds create loud sounds, soft winds/soft sounds, wind stops/pauses in cymbal patterns.) Dance steps in meandering floor patterns, and spins and turns echo the theme of something carried by the wind. Large, abstract gestures contrasted with small arm movements, reflecting changes in the music and echoing the theme of strong winds alternating with soft winds.
Notes: I danced this piece as an improvisation, then outlined the choreography. I selected music after creating the choreography outline, adapting the pacing and the steps to fit the selected song. In this case, the music was the setting for the dance. The movements were designed to fit the interests and skill level of the group who commissioned the choreography.

Example 2: One of my students designed a veil dance for her own youthful group of 15 dancers

OPPOSITE: *Ramona in a modern interpretive belly dance performance. The fan motif reflects the telenovela-inspired theme (Spanish language soap opera). Additional motifs include Spanish dance steps and modern dance floorwork fused with traditional belly dance movements. The accompanying music was a guitar instrumental. (Photo by Bob Winn Photography.)*

to perform for a Christmas celebration at a church.[19] While this was not classic belly dance, it included belly dance veil techniques. However, this same set of steps, adapted with different costuming, different music, and different intent, could be performed in a classic belly dance style. Dance steps are like a vocabulary; steps can express many different ideas. Ideas for her dance included:

Theme: Angels are celebrating Christmas

Motifs: Veil movements and floor patterns expressing the theme (veil draped to resemble angels' wings, veil held like a baby, veil held upward with hands open toward heaven, star-shaped floor pattern)

Music: Preselected by church music department; mostly instrumental song, with verses singing "Glory" and short segments of vocals about the Christmas story (echoing the theme)

Costumes: All white leotards and tights, full skirts, veils (echoing "Angels" theme)

Choreography: Floor patterns: star shape (echoing the theme), straight lines, wavy lines. Movement patterns in aisles: individual "angels" dancing as soloists. Stage area: solo dances in a round robin format; group of "angels" dancing onstage in a pinwheel and other formations. Dance steps: simple traveling steps and use of "big" veil movements, veils held high (echoing the theme). Gestures: a veil held like a baby; palms together in prayer position; arms open in V position, referencing upwards toward heaven (illustrating some of the words in the song).

Exercises:

Note to teachers: The first two exercises below are useful for belly dance "circuit training" in class. In a workshop, I posted signs on the walls around the room with a few of the cues from these two exercises. Students selected a geometric shape to use as a motif, then formed a single-file line and danced through the circuit, following the posted signs on the stations for varying their motif, and ending with a pose at the end of the circuit. It's fun for all levels of students, and helps students link different movements and vary a motif within a dance.

Using movement motifs: Select a geometric shape, combination of steps, or floor pattern to use as a motif. (Examples: circle, 3-step turn plus a finger snap or square floor pattern.) Next, dance the motif in any of the following ways, creating new variations of the way you use a familiar dance movement:

- Do half the motif and pause for effect
- Dance the motif very slowly
- Dance the motif very quickly
- Dance the motif with the upper body only
- Dance the motif backwards
- Group motif (example: duet with each dancer doing half the movement or pattern)
- Dance the motif at an angle

Isolations with geometric motifs: Geometric shapes are frequently used as isolated dance movements of the head, shoulders, ribs, hips or feet. Select one of the following geometric patterns: circle, triangle, S-curve, star, square, spiral or any other geometry. Next, dance the pattern with the following variations:

- Use motif as a floor pattern
- Dance motif with one shoulder
- Trace motif with hands
- Dance motif with hips
- Draw motif upside down and dance it with hand or hip
- Draw sideways motif with wrist or hip
- Dance half the motif and pause for effect
- Draw motif overhead with hands

OPPOSITE: *Playing finger cymbals adds liveliness and fun to dances performed with recorded music. (Photo of Ramona.)*

Selecting a prop can be a starting point for new choreography and improvisation ideas. Photo of Sadira Mahin with her sword.

- Space hold motif (hands stay in place, as if holding something with one hand or two hands, while drawing the motif as a floor pattern by stepping. You can visualize red paint on the soles of the feet leaving a trail of the motif behind, while hands stay firmly in place.)
- Motif as floorwork (reclining, kneeling or sitting while hands or feet "draw" motif)
- Motif as a group (example: a duet with each dancer doing half the floor pattern)
- Body hold motif (hold a pose while drawing the motif by turning or walking a floor pattern) (Example: arms holding a V position while walking a complete circular floor pattern/motif.)

You will not necessarily use all these ideas in your dance, but they serve as building blocks for establishing the foundation of your dance. Remember to add contrasting movements for variety in a complete dance. For example, if your movements are mainly S-curves, you could use angular, staccato movements for contrast.

Theme and motif: Select a theme, story, or scenario. (Examples: modern belly dance, folkloric, tribal style themes, or a scenario or storyline.) Next, answer the following questions:

- What music would go with your theme?
- What costume style would you wear?

- Would a prop enhance your dance? If so, what would go with your theme?
- What dance movements would you use to fit the theme?
- Which dance movements would you repeat?
- Which movements would be highlights in your dance?
- What movements would you use for contrasts and transitions?

Prop as a motif: Sometimes a prop is a starting point for creating a dance. Ideas for a dance may emerge from a storyline or idea related to the prop. Select a prop and music, then improvise a dance to see what develops. Here are some useful props for belly dance performances (see Resources for vendors of specialty props):

- Fringed shawl
- Mask
- Hat
- Cane
- Veil (or multiple veils)
- Scarves
- Spanish fan, Oriental fan or feather fan
- Melaya (Egyptian ladies' wrap, a large black shawl)
- Candles (tea lights, votives, oil or battery-operated candles in decorative holders)
- Tray (holding candles, flowers, perfumes or other decor)
- Belly dance sword, sabre or scimitar (blunt edged and balanced for dancing)[20]
- Candleabra (Egyptian headpiece and candles for *raqs shamadan*)
- Coins (used for flipping and rolling on the belly)
- Isis wings
- Waterglasses (the dancer stands on the glasses)[21]
- Basket, pitcher or wineglass[22]
- Plush, rubber or battery-operated snakes for comedy dances. (A live snake is a dance partner, not a prop!)

Balancing a prop: Looking in a mirror, place your prop (start with a lightweight, unbreakable basket or tray) on your head and get it in a position where it balances. After it's comfortably balanced, put your hands on the prop, as if to remove it. Pause, noticing precisely where your hands are placed, and the angle of your arms. Next, remove the prop and again place it on your head, this time putting your arms in the position that you just observed in the mirror. With practice, you will be able to balance the prop without the mirror.

I had difficulty balancing my belly dance sword, until I saw that my forearm and upper arm made an L shape when the sword was placed in the correct position. Putting the arm in the correct position is faster and easier than trying to find the balance point on the prop, and then adjusting it until it balances. The position of your arms will vary according to the prop you are using.

You can make balancing easier by gluing a non-skid fabric to the bottom of your prop (especially for flat-bottom props like baskets, candles and trays).

Some dancers make balancing easier by wearing a padded headband or scarf. If you do not wear a headpiece, a generous amount of hair spray or other tacky-textured hair product will help your hair be less slippery. However, do not use hair spray when dancing with candles or other fire dances, since hair spray is flammable! Costumes for fire dances must be nonflammable too.

CHAPTER SIX

Developing Movement Combinations and Choreography

"There is nothing more notable in Socrates than that he found time, when he was an old man, to learn music and dancing, and thought it time well spent."

MICHEL DE MONTAIGNE (1533–1592), RENAISSANCE SCHOLAR

I believe that dancers of all skill levels benefit from learning innovative choreography. Learning other people's choreographed dances was a necessary step for me, which helped me create my own dances later.

In this section, we'll look at how to get started, understanding beats, and these approaches to creating dances:

- *Intuitive approach*
- *Dancing the music approach*
- *Select movements first approach*
- *Jump right in approach*
- *Backdoor approach*

Getting started

There is no "right" or "wrong" way to go about creating dances. The best approach is the one which works for *you*. The solution to creating choreography and improvisations faster and better is to choose a *theme*. There are many approaches, but generally they involve:

- Selecting your music, then selecting your approach to dancing with that music, letting the music guide you into a theme, *or*
- Selecting your theme first, letting the dance steps evolve from the theme and merging movements with the music.

OPPOSITE: *Coco performing a high-energy cabaret veil dance.*
Example of a cabaret theme with a veil motif.

Here are some ideas for getting started with developing an approach:

- Select songs from various CDs, improvise movements and see what develops.
- Select a scenario or storyline to act out, then select music to accompany that idea.
- Select music that establishes a certain mood and let movements evolve.
- Listen to music as you go to sleep (for some people, this results in having choreography ideas upon awakening).
- Listen to music, and a visualization of the dance spontaneously comes to you.
- Make a commentary about a person, place or thing through dance (acting out a character or creating a dance about a subject).

The first step is to select the outline or plan you want to use, just the way a good writer does. The plan a dancer uses is not necessarily written down (though many dancers like written notes). Writers use outlines and themes, and many choreographers also use this method (either written or memorized).

Many belly dance choreographers use themes. By using a theme, you will save time creating choreography. Using a theme during an improvisation helps a dancer choose what step to do next during the dance, which helps the dance flow.

Personally, I found that using a theme cut the time I was spending creating choreography in half. I also felt more confident with dancing by improvisation. Using a theme makes the process more fun, and the resulting dances more beautiful.

At times, the theme is not apparent to the audience, as in an abstract dance. The result that the audience sees is a dance which flows well and has a cohesive design (instead of a dance which is put together without a framework.)

Understanding beats

Beats is a familiar term in music, but "beats" also has meanings related to dance and language. "Beats" in written language refer to changes which push a storyline or scenario along, just as changing patterns in a song move the musical story along. Dances also have beats, which are changes that move the choreography or improvisation forward.

Script writers and authors use beats in their work. A television news writer may have a story consisting of the following beats: the writer tells us generally about weather (beat 1, introducing the story); then gives us details of the forecast (beat 2, change in the story, giving us details). The writer choreographs the words, and a weather reporter recites them.

Abstract and storytelling dances also have beats which develop the story. Here is a brief example of beats used in belly dance:

- 16-count movement combination based on hip circles and hand claps *(beat 1)*.
- Different 16-count combination of movements based on rib circles *(beat 2)*.
- New combination of movements based on a square floor pattern *(beat 3)*.

Each change moves the dance along. A detailed example of a "beat analysis" used in a storyline dance is in the Appendix.

Intuitive approach

Some choreographers are blessed with a highly-developed intuition that enables them to *"listen to the music and the dance just comes."* [23] Some dancers construct wonderful choreography and improvisations this way.

This approach doesn't work for everyone, though many dancers get brief flashes of inspiration. If the intuitive approach to dancemaking doesn't give you the whole dance, it's still important to pay attention to your intuitions and flashes of inspiration. You will find these moments of intuition helpful while using more scripted methods of creating dances.

Dancing the music approach

Dancing the music begins with selecting a song. Then, you let the song guide you into a theme. The song's mood, tempo, lyrics, and/or instruments inspire you to select dance movements. For example, a "happy" feeling song would evoke light-hearted, happy dance movements like hops, moderate tempo steps, and big gestures.

Some choreographers literally dance the lyrics to the song, using gestures. For example, in a song where the singer was saying *"no, no, no,"* an Egyptian choreographer shakes her head and uses a finger-wagging gesture for emphasis. Many choreographers are less literal, and create dances based on the general mood of the music.

If you feel the tone of the song is "serious," facial expressions and body movements will be different from dancing a "happy" dance with energetic steps and hops. For example, an American choreographer created a troupe dance to an Egyptian love song with lyrics *"my eye will remember you"* using an eye-shaped floor pattern. The general mood of the veil dance was soft and repetitive, reflecting the general meaning of the lyrics, rather than acting out the words.

Another approach is to dance to the main melody, main instruments or percussion. A contrasting approach is to dance to the subtleties of the music (rather than the main melody or louder instruments which dominate the music). Here is an example:

I interviewed my friend Oracle, choreographer and director of metro Atlanta's popular tribal fusion troupe *Dance of the Fates*, regarding a fire

and sword dance which her trio performed using this approach. Oracle said that she started by selecting music which inspired her, then created choreography by selecting movements which fit the subtleties of the music. She said that it feels right to add or change props when there are major changes in the music. Using this approach, she created a dance which was part trio (with all the dancers moving in unison), part duet and part solo. This dance has many interesting changes, effective use of music, and creative use of props.

Movements first approach

In this approach, you begin by selecting your favorite movements and steps, or floor patterns, or other specific elements to include in your dance. You identify which movements you want to use, and then look for a song they fit. Using preselected steps in improvisational dances is useful during dance classes; students follow the teacher's movements, or teachers call out cues while students practice the movements.

I recently wanted to teach a specific movement combination (hip circle, rib circle, shoulder circle). To put this into a choreographed dance, I listened to several songs until I found appropriate music. I adapted the movements to fit the music better, making them big, small, fast and slow, and including pauses to fit the music.

Songs with repetitive musical phrases work well for helping students practice and repeat a particular combination. Repetition helps students remember the sequence of movements and reinforces the learning process. Practicing the same movement combinations to different music selections is also important, because it shows us how to vary speed, feeling and musical interpretation.

To finish this choreography or improvisation, your movements need to be adapted and timed so that they mesh with the music. You can do this by

Beautiful Mahira showing a perfect pose for a hip drop. By facing the audience at an angle, the arms frame the body to clearly show the hip movement. When a dancer uses the "select movements first" approach, she must position herself to show the selected movement.

making movements big, small, fast or slow, and by including pauses for emphasis that coincide with the music. Transitions between movement combinations are important to link the dance together and help it "flow." Remember to include contrasting movements, highlights (movements which stand out, including pauses), and climactic points (poses or accents) to your dance for variety. For an improvisational or solo dance, the dancer can spontaneously make changes during the performance and adapt it to the feeling of the moment.

Some dancers first develop a theme or storyline for the dance, choreograph steps, then work with a musician to develop music to fit this theme, or select existing music to fit the theme. The dance does not interpret the music; instead, the music is the setting for the dance.

Here is an analogy:

A movie actress recites her lines (choreographed words) while background music emphasizes the meaning of her words, gestures and facial expressions. For example, a tension-building scene includes music which builds anticipation and suspense; a comic scene uses music which sounds humorous. The music adds to the effect and intent of the spoken words (or dance movements), gestures and facial expressions. The music is the setting for the action; the actress (or dancer) is not interpreting the music.

Belly dance choreographers, as well as choreographers in other dance genres, often use the theme-first approach. You may choreograph an elegant, dramatic or comic dance, then select music to set the scene which enhances the elegant, dramatic or humorous theme of the selected dance movements. You can adapt the dance steps to fit the music and show the skills and strengths of the dancer(s) performing the piece.

Jump right in approach

The "jump right in" approach is the way some dancers go about creating choreography:

- A dancer decides to create a choreographed dance.
- Next they select music, and then
- "Jump right in" with selecting dance movements to fit the music:
  - Create one dance phrase (example, 8 counts of movement).
  - Contemplate it, decide it needs some changes, so they revise it.
  - Select more movements (example, 16 counts).
  - Revise again.
  - The rest of the creative flow follows this process.
  - Eventually the dance is finished.

This approach is more difficult than some of the others, but since many dancers use it, understanding its problems and pitfalls is important. The key problem with jumping right in is that it generally takes far too long, because the dance is without a theme or direction. Going one choreographic phrase (combination of steps, usually counted 8's) at a time, is time-consuming.

Just as rewriting and editing a letter countless times is a frustrating experience, so it is with the "jump right in" approach to choreography. Dancers who use this approach have told me that they find creating choreography very time-consuming and frustrating.

Another significant problem with jumping right into choreography is that the results may not fit the overall structure of the music. The phrase-by-phrase approach may result in a dance without a cohesive theme.

For example, I recall a group choreography created in a class I attended many years ago. Each dancer created a combination, then we put all the combinations into a dance. Although we accurately counted every beat, there was no overall theme to the dance. The result was choppy and difficult for the dancers to memorize, since there were no repeating steps to link the dance together. This is analogous to writing an email or a letter without a clearly stated purpose; there is no overall direction in which you're going. Without a theme, a dance may wind up as scrabble rather than communication.

A third problem with creating a dance phrase-by-phrase is that this approach may stifle creativity. Dancers and teachers are often working under deadlines to create a dance for a particular event, such as a workshop or special public performance. They know that creating choreography is a time-consuming process. Under the pressure of time, they fall into using familiar movements in familiar patterns or previously-created choreographic phrases (combinations) to save time, rather than creating something new. Using a theme helps you put together movements in a new way.

Backdoor approach (What to do when you don't know where to start)

You're listening to a favorite song and hear a segment that sounds like a hip shimmy. So you know that you're going to shimmy at that point in the music, but you don't have ideas about what to do with the rest of the song. What do you do? It's time for the "backdoor approach," which means that we start by selecting movements and listening to the music, then later figure out the theme.

First, listen to the song to identify its structure and where segments begin and end. Grouping into segments is useful, because it breaks a song up into small segments. You can start by choreographing any segment, rather than trying to figure out how to choreograph an entire song from start to finish, one choreographic phrase at a time. We're breaking up the task into small bites, instead of tackling one big sandwich:

- Identify where the introductory segment ends.
- Listen to the music several times to identify changes (beats) in the song (naming them A, B, C, etc.). Identify segments by rhythm, tempo, musical instruments or vocal accompaniment. For example, call a segment of flute and clarinet "A" (wind instruments); a fast percussive section "B" (drums). Or, if the song has vocals, call the soloist "A," the instrumental "B," and the chorus "C." Note a new letter at each significant change. If you hear an exact or almost-exact repetition, give it the same designation as the previous time you heard it (such as ABA). Simplify your notation as much as possible.
- Which musical phrases repeat? Notice where phrases repeat. Listen for other sounds which suggest specific movements to you, and note in which segment they appear and where they repeat.
- Go to the beginning of the song, and figure out how you're going to get on stage. Do you want to travel on stage or begin already there? Fast forward to the end and listen to what the music suggests to you. Do you want to travel offstage while the music fades, or end with a pose? Improvise dance movement and note what works with the music and the feelings you want to express.
- You've outlined some ideas for the beginning, middle and end of the dance. Next, listen to the music and note on paper what each segment "feels" like to you. Perhaps you feel the melody segment as "flowing," and maybe a percussive section feels like it calls for "snappy" movements. You may find that making your notes as scribbled diagrams helps; if certain parts of the music feel wavy or linear to you, draw a sketch to describe it. Improvise dance movements and note what feels right to you.
- Look for *motifs*. Review the movements you selected to see what they have in common, and notice where they contrast. Now you can link movements within segments by using different movements with the same *shapes*. Improvise again and note what works.

  For example, in a "flowing" section you could begin with an undulating arm movement (motif). A possibility for continuing with the flow of the music might be to travel with a simple walking step in an undulating, S-curving floor pattern. By doing this you've transferred the undulating shape to the floor. During the "vibrating" section of the music, you may perform your hip shimmy or vibration (a new motif). Later, as the music changes, transfer the shimmy to your shoulders or hands. There are limitless possibilities.
- Look for your *theme*. Review what you have so far, and see what patterns are repeating. You may find that a particular set of steps or geometric patterns dominate your dance (examples: S-curving theme, circular theme). Or, your dance and music may have an overall feeling that suggests its theme. (Examples: Turkish theme, celebration theme, fusion theme.)

After completing your choreography, dance it several times and make whatever changes you feel are appropriate. If you are a teacher, ensure that the difficulty of the dance matches the class level you are teaching. Beginner level dances need to be more repetitive and use simpler movements than dances for the intermediate and advanced levels.

Polishing your dance: establishing a motif and a theme

Review the movements in your dance, looking for common elements. Is your dance dominated by circular movements, such as hip circles, shoulder circles, and circular floor patterns? Are there gaps in your choreography?

Using a *theme* (main idea of a dance: storyline, design idea, step combination or other idea) and a *motif* (prop, floor pattern, body movements, steps, or other elements which evoke the theme) will help you finish your dance and give it cohesion. A circle is an example of a useful theme for a dance. Motifs could be circular floor patterns, and could be varied by transforming the circle into a spiral floor pattern later in the dance.

Another example of a theme could be your favorite set of steps repeated in a dance, but done with variations: directional changes, tempo changes, and varying steps from big to small, and adding pauses between steps.

Choosing a theme and motif(s) depends on your personal preferences and interpretation of the music. That is, when you listen to the music, does it generally "feel" flowing, angular, pulsating, undulating, etc.? Does it remind you of a story, scenario or character? These may also be used as themes to build a dance on.

If you're stuck for ideas, doodle on a sheet of paper while listening, then look at your doodle to see whether you had flowing lines, curving shapes, or angles.

The idea is to listen to the music and determine what kind of feeling it evokes; to translate sound from airwaves to a visual picture, which eventually evolves into a dance. If you've already partially completed a dance via the backdoor approach, the movements you've selected so far may already show your underlying theme and motif.

Choreography is a combined effort

If you perform someone else's choreography, inform your audience who created it, either in the MC's announcement or in the written program. Although choreography is often one person's interpretation of a song, the dancer performing it puts her own emotional and expressive stamp on it.

A Georgia instructor says that she has a particular student who performs her dances *"better than I do (myself)."* A choreography you learn from someone else has a synergy; it is a combination of the choreographer's art, plus *your* personal energy, expression and interpretation. It is a combination of two people's artistic interpretations.

Choreography is for all levels of dancers. Elite performers in the U.S. and the Middle East have choreographers who design dances for their shows, in the same manner that ballet companies have choreographers. Nagwa Fouad of Egypt worked with choreographer Mohammed Khalil for years to create great dances. Their *combined* artistry resulted in dances that made her the "Queen of Oriental Dance."[24]

Exercises:

Step-by-step: Use an idea from this chapter or, using one of your own ideas, select a:

> *Theme, Scenario or Storyline* (story tells who, what, why, when, where and how).
> *Motif* (dance step, combination, symbol, prop or other element that evokes the theme).
> *Music* (which evokes the theme).
> *Costume* (which evokes the theme).
> *Choreography* or *plan for improvisation* (which evokes the theme).

Easy Group Dance: Select a song you can count in 8's. Select four simple movements, then weave them into a dance using:

- Traveling steps in any floor pattern.
- Movement standing in place.
- Traveling steps in a different direction.
- End the sequence with an in-place movement.
- Repeat the entire sequence throughout the music, ending with a group pose.
- Changing speed, body level, or other elements during repetitions adds variety.

If you find the Easy Dance idea useful, try adapting it to various floor patterns and movements. You could perform it as a line dance, a dance in the round, a figure 8 floor pattern, or other pattern. Endless variations are possible.

More ideas for easy group dances: The cross-cultural idea of simple dances dates from ancient times. Many cultures have traditions of group dances in circular formations which have evolved and are still performed today. Some of these dances use standard sets of steps which fit multiple songs.

Growing up in West Virginia, I learned numerous square dance step patterns, which fit a variety of songs. Square dances sometimes have a "caller" who calls out cues for step patterns. This format is also adaptable to belly dance; an effective class exercise is to call out names of various movements and have students practice the steps, weaving them into a dance in a wavy, linear or circular floor pattern.

Backdoor approach: Following directions in this chapter, create a dance using the backdoor approach. Listen to a song or instrumental and let it tell you what it wants your dance to be like! Choose a:

> *Theme* (main idea) or *Storyline* (telling a story of who, what, why, when, where and how).
> *Motif* (dance movement(s), symbol, prop or other element that evokes the theme).
> *Music* (which evokes the theme).
> *Costume* (which evokes the theme).
> *Choreography* or *plan for improvisation* (which evokes the theme).

OPPOSITE: *Choreography is a synergistic effort between the dancer and choreographer. Ramona in a theatrical performance of a choreography by Dalia.*

CHAPTER SEVEN

Proven Methods of Creating Dynamic Dances

"That which cannot be spoken, can be sung.
That which cannot be sung, can be danced"

FRENCH SAYING

*D*ance is the personal, nonverbal, abstract language of body movement. Just as there are proven methods of writing business letters, making speeches and carrying on conversations, there are proven methods of creating dances.

There are many ways to coordinate movement with music to create dances, but there is no "right way" or "wrong way" to create dances. The best way is the way that works for *you*. Here are some of the structures used for creating improvised and choreographed dances:

- *Improvisation*
- *Collage*
- *Binary (AB)*
- *Ternary (ABA)*
- *Verse and chorus*
- *Rondo*
- *Theme and variations*
- *Storytelling/narrative*
- *Novelty*
- *Comedy*

This is *not* a comprehensive list, but a place to start. A method may be used on its own, or combined with another method to create a dance.

An important concept to remember is the *primacy* and *recency effects*. The beginning and ending of a song or dance will be remembered more than what happened in the middle. Therefore, it's important for a dancer to start strong and end strong. When memorizing a choreographed dance, it usually takes more effort to remember the series of steps in the middle than to remember the beginning and the ending. Audiences also tend to remember the beginning, ending, highlights and climactic points more than the other movements in your dance.

OPPOSITE: *Poses and pauses provide contrast to flowing movements within dances. (Photo of Ramona.)*

Improvisation

Improvising movements to a selected song is a familiar experience for dancers. Listening to music inspires dancers to select movements that go along with the music. Another approach is to preselect movements to practice, then make them fit the music by adapting the speed of the steps and including pauses for effect. A common approach to creating choreography is to be inspired by the music, improvising movements, and then memorize the sequence of movements for future use.

Collage

A *collage* in visual art refers to a collection of diverse design elements (for example, multiple photographs of different subjects), which are framed together as one. A dance collage is a collection of different movement phrases, or combinations of steps, which are framed together into a dance with a beginning, middle and ending. The central idea is a collection of diverse images that come together into one dance. Collage dances may be performed as solos or in troupes, choreographed or improvised. These are also called *round robins* when performed by sequential dancers.

Example 1:

- Each dancer in a group selects a movement of her choice.
- Dancer #1 dances her movement for a few counts.
- Dancer #2 dances her movement for a few counts.
- Dancer #3 dances, and so on.

Having each dancer link her movement with the previous movement makes this exercise cohesive. For example, using a specific gesture to indicate passing on to the next dancer's turn, or having the dancers repeat a previous dance movement before demonstrating their own movement choice.

Example 2, favored by some dancers as their preferred method of creating collages for solo or group performances:

- Select movement combinations (sets of steps/movements, usually counted in 8's).
- Put them together.
- Add smooth transitions between combinations to make the dance cohesive.

Collage of different floor patterns and design ideas for hand, hip and arm or other isolated body movements.

Some teachers give specific movement combinations descriptive or memorable names, to help students remember sets of movements better. (Example: "chocolate and mint combo" refers to a prescribed sequence of veil dance movements.) It's handy to label combinations for easier recall.

Binary (AB format)

A *binary* dance consists of two sections of contrasting feeling. One way to do this is to select different parts of the body to highlight in each section. For simplicity, we call the sections "A" and "B."

Example:

A: Ney (flute); accompanied by the dancer's delicate hand movements.
B: Drum solo; the dancer focuses on strong hip movements.

Ternary (ABA format)

A *ternary* dance consists of three segments. It is similar to binary, but with a third segment which is similar to the beginning of the dance, resulting in an ABA format. The ending segment nicely rounds out the dance and links the improvisation or choreography together. It is more artistically pleasing than the binary format.

Example:

A: A flowing section of movements with a veil.
B: The veil is discarded and the focus is on precise hip articulations.
A: The veil is retrieved and flowing movements follow, and the dance ends with a pose.

Verse and chorus

Just as many songs are composed of verses alternating with a repeating chorus, a dance may be composed the same way. This type of choreography is called *question and answer, call and response* or *call and reply,* because it feels like a conversation.

A solo dancer may perform both roles (selecting one type of movement to be the verse, and a different set of movements as the chorus). Another possibility is having a solo dancer perform the verse, with a supporting group of dancers as a chorus line.

Or, there could be multiple groups of dancers. A duo could dance the verse, and another duo could dance the chorus in call-and-response style, facing each other in two lines.

Example:

Verse: phrase of movement (hip drop and finger snap movement combination).
Chorus: different combination of movements/ steps (traveling steps).
New verse: new dance movements with a similar feeling as the first verse (hip drop and hip snap combination).
Chorus: exact or similar repetition of previous chorus (repeat traveling steps).

Rondo

A *rondo* is a variation of the verse and chorus format. Instead of exact or similar repetitions of verses and choruses, repeating segments are interspersed with totally new material. For example, if a dance combination with hip lifts is "A," floorwork is "B," flowing arm movements are "C," and a taqsim is "D," an example of Rondo would be: A B A C A D A.

Theme and variations

Egyptian choreographer Mahmoud Reda remarked that, just as a dancer would not want to put every color into one costume, too many movements in one dance make it too busy. It is better to base a dance on a few movements, and to use interesting variations of these movements.[25] This approach is called *theme and variations.*

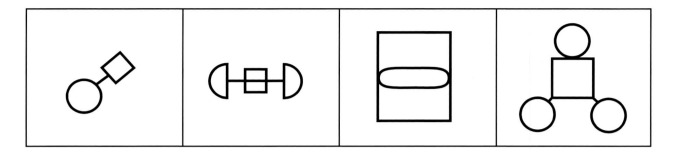

A theme and variations. Designs for floor patterns for traveling steps, or for hand, hip, shoulder or other isolated movements.

This method involves a recurring theme (basic series of movements) which is continuously adapted throughout the dance. By the end of the dance, the original theme has been varied so much that it appears very different from the beginning of the dance. However, at the end of the dance, the basic style of the original theme is still there. There is an element of the variations which relate to the original theme. For example, if the beginning of a dance has a curving floor pattern, the end of the dance also has a curving pattern, although all the dance movements continuously change throughout the piece.

To choreograph using a theme and variations, a series of movements is selected. Then, you continuously adapt this series of movements.

Here is an example of adapting a theme into several variations:

- Select a motif, for example, a circle and a square shape *(theme)*.
- Draw the circle and square with your hips *(motif)*.
- Draw the circle and square with your hands overhead *(variation)*.
- Draw a circle and square on the floor with your toe *(variation)*.
- Travel in a spiral floor pattern (a modified circle), then in a square pattern *(variation)*.
- Make a figure 8 (two circles) with your hands in front of your body *(variation)*.

- Make a figure 8 variation, creating two hip squares instead of circles *(variation)*.

A choreography or improvisation composed of a theme and variations might show simple dance combinations evolving gradually into more challenging combinations, or be based on a sequence of combinations that show basic hip and shoulder movements changing into hand and head movements, then into foot and knee movements. Transferring a movement from one part of the body to another is a proven way of creating variations.

Storytelling and narrative dances

Do you have a favorite story? Think about embellishing it for a short presentation on stage. A storyline is a structured telling of a tale (with or without narration, acted out in dance). Or, it is a private storyline which inspires a series of movements and results in a beautiful abstract dance.

Telling a story sometimes requires an explanation to the audience; make sure you give the master of ceremonies an introductory write-up explaining your dance if you want the meaning of your dance to be obvious. Effective use of appropriate props and setting the stage are also helpful with storytelling.

This type of dance is very entertaining, and is useful in dramatic dances, novelty dances and comic dances. An advantage of a storytelling dance is that you already have a built-in plot, complete with an introduction, highlights, climactic point and ending. Shows during dance workshops and retreats frequently include a performance or two of this type of dance. Both soloists and groups can tell stories effectively.

Examples:

• Coco (pictured) entered the stage dressed as a princess, complete with a crown and elaborate purple robe, accompanied by two "ladies in waiting." A throne and other props set the stage. The "princess" opened a sparkling box, and she transformed into a belly dancer. At the end of her dance, she went back into her princess persona and regally carried the "magical" box off stage.

• An Atlanta troupe danced with a "camel" (two people dressed in a camel costume), a "sultan," and a cast of dancers. The cast led the camel on the stage and the group showed their story in a dance.

• Another effective performance showed a woman acting out her life in dance. She first showed us tap dancing (acting as a young girl), later square dancing, waddling as a pregnant woman, and going on to mimic giving birth, motherhood, and ending as a belly dancer. Two assistants on stage handed her various props for each persona, and she used an appropriate musical accompaniment for each different segment. It was a humorous storytelling dance that was very entertaining.

Coco in scenes from her "Dance of the Princess" performed in Atlanta, Georgia.

Storytelling dances are as much fun for the performer as they are for the audience. Another positive aspect of this type of dance is that the dancing itself is usually easy. Complicated dance steps and body movements are generally not necessary for this type of dance. However, if you want to use challenging movements, you could include them if they fit with the storyline.

"Show, don't tell," is frequent advice given to fiction writers (storytellers). This advice also applies to storytelling dances. "Show, don't tell" means avoiding too much narration of the story. Let the characters show the story, not the narrator.

However, use a narrator if you need one. A narrator can help set the scene and tell us the time and place of your story. A storytelling dance will not be successful if the audience doesn't know you're telling a story. For example, if you want your props to "talk," they'll need a voice.

Novelty and comic dances

Novelty and comic dances don't necessarily tell a story, but they show a character or employ an unusual prop. People dressed as dancing camels are an example. Two students performed such a dance at a theatrical show several years ago, complete with cymbals attached to the knees and played by the camel! These dances are fun for the audience and the performers. Here is another example of a novelty dance:

> In the "Dance of the Four Directions" (North, South, East, and West), four dancers each played a role. My role was to do the "Dance of the South." I decided to be a Southern Belle belly dancer. The costume was a frothy pink skirt and veil, pink and white top and belt, a parasol, and 1860's style pink hat with a feather. The music was "Georgia on my mind."[26]

There is an abundance of ideas for novelty and comic dances. Audiences usually enjoy these performances in theatrical venues such as dance concerts, student recitals and theatrical shows.

When creating novelty and comic dances, it is a good idea to get an opinion from another person (not necessarily a dancer) before dancing it onstage. Friends can give valuable feedback, since they see the total picture.

In order for a comic or novelty dance to be understood, the meaning of the dance *must* be clear to the audience. A comedy dance must be obviously funny, and a novelty dance must use appropriate music to coordinate with the props and costuming, in order for the audience to get the point.

Dance is a three-way communication: the *dancer* and her accompanying *music* communicate an idea or story to the *audience*, and the audience responds with their attention and applause.

Additional examples

Some of the dances mentioned in this chapter used simple movement patterns, while others were more complicated. There is a beauty to both styles; simplicity has an elegance to it, and complexity takes us into a level of sophistication. Here are additional examples of performances and structures I've seen on stage:

- Postcard images of Lebanon (veil dance solo) *(collage choreography)*
- Modern Egyptian solo dance *(improvisation)*
- Drum solo (folkloric Egyptian troupe dance) *(theme and variations choreography)*
- Cymbal dance with cymbals acting out characters (boy cymbal had a blue ribbon tied to it, girl cymbal had pink ribbon) *(novelty dance choreography)*
- Greek dramas, music, architecture, Byzantine flavor solo *(collage choreography)*
- Modern belly dance to upbeat Egyptian pop song *(call and reply troupe choreography)*

- Modern interpretive belly dance solo *(ternary improvisation)*
- Troupe members dance to a classic song *(rondo choreography)*

Exercises:

Collage: Each of us has many aspects to our personality. Create a dance based on aspects of your individuality. Stay in character for each segment. (Example: if you are involved with learning Turkish, Egyptian, and ballet movements, you could weave segments of each of these movement styles together. Example 2: if you want to express a "celebration" feeling, be "wild" and express "shyness," you could create a dance with segments evoking these feelings in turn.)

Ternary: Select two movements or steps (or two movement combinations), designating them A and B. Then dance them in this sequence: A B A.

Verse and chorus: Select two movements (or two movement combinations), designating them A and B. Select a song. Dance your selected movements in the following sequence: A B A B A. Vary A and B by changing arm positions and floor patterns during repetitions.

Theme and variations: Select a geometric shape (such as a circle, square or triangle), then dance it with different parts of the body. (Example: using a circle, start by drawing the circle with fingertips, then with shoulders, elbows, walk it as a floor pattern, trace it with a toe, one hip, both hips.) This is a basic way of varying a theme. Next, using this shape, let it evolve into variations. Experiment with making your selected movements or pattern:

- Bigger
- Smaller
- Faster
- Slower

- Retrograde (perform the floor pattern or steps in reverse)
- Vary the direction of steps or movements
- Add pauses for effect

Storytelling/narrative: Dance a story or scenario, nonverbally acting out *who, what, why, when, where* and *how* the action takes place. Think of someone in history, legend, or mythology who interests you. How would you base a dance on this character? How would you set the stage? What props would you use? What story would you act out? What are your introduction, highlights, and climactic points of this dance story?

Novelty dance: Do you have a favorite character from history, a novel or a drama? Could this character be acted out in a dance? What props would you use?

Comedy dance: Create a character from an animal (camels are fun, but there are lots of other choices too). Another option is to use an object (maybe a veil?) as your "character." How would you make it humorous? How would it dance? What would it say? How would you introduce the dance? What music would best suit this dance? Improvise your introduction, highlights, and climactic point of this dance story.

Rondo: Select movements or movement combinations you already know, labeling them A, B, C, D. Select a song. Next, dance your selected movements in the following sequence: A B A C A D A.

Suite: Select slow, medium, and fast movements, and select a song (or songs). Dance your selected movements in the following sequence: medium tempo introduction, slow middle section, fast finale.

Dance of the Fates troupe moving in unison. From left: Liora, Fatina and Oracle.

CHAPTER EIGHT

Special Considerations for Group Dances

*"You give but little when you give of your possessions.
It is when you give of yourself that you truly give."*

KAHLIL GIBRAN (1883–1931), LEBANESE-AMERICAN AUTHOR

Many dancers prefer dancing in a group, and troupe dances are fun for audiences to watch too. Besides the elements that pertain to dancing as a soloist, there are additional considerations for dancing with others in a duo, trio or troupe. Dance style, organization and level of technical difficulty need to be considered when designing a group dance.

Creating and performing dances with a group is a collaborative experience. Some groups create choreography and improvisations with input from everyone, whereas others have a choreographer who sets the dance routine and teaches it to the group. Everyone in the group works together in rehearsing and smoothing out the dance.

Choreography for groups

One opinion voiced by a troupe director is that choreography for groups should be at the difficulty level of the performer with the *least* expertise. A dance which is too challenging makes for stressful performances. An easy troupe choreography is sometimes more impressive to watch than a more difficult one, since the easy dance will be more polished, and the less experienced students can shine because they are more relaxed.

Another approach used by some choreographers is to challenge their dancers with more complex choreography to build skill level. This is good for dance classes, and when the students have mastered the technically challenging dance, they can perform it with confidence.

What makes a dance easy? Few steps, uncomplicated movements and a short piece of fabulous music. Interesting floor patterns and variations of movements add spice without increasing the difficulty level too much.

For public performances, it is best to separate intermediate and advanced level students into separate troupes, and to have each group use dances choreographed for their level of expertise. Differences in skill level are particularly apparent with duets and small groups.

Even the dances for the advanced and professional level troupes should be made somewhat easier than their actual skill levels, so that the resulting performance will appear polished and effortless. The general level of difficulty will be much higher for advanced level performers, since their overall skill level is also higher.

Additional considerations for designing group dances:

- *Big solo or different parts*
- *Group improvisation*
- *Random*
- *Ripple (canon, fugue)*

Big solo or different parts

Many group dances are actually big solos: the dancers all perform the same steps at the same time, and dance on the stage together in a group. Usually a group of dancers doing the same movements simultaneously are dressed alike or similarly, giving them a unified appearance. This approach is very common in belly dance and in other dance forms. The opposite approach is to have individual dancers doing different things, such as being different characters in a storytelling dance, or having a group dance be part duet, part solo, and part trio.

I recently watched choreographed performances by two renowned professional belly dance companies. I observed that these troupes performed steps and movements that the choreographers, when dancing as soloists, preferred. This is not surprising, since dance teachers naturally instruct their students in the stylization and steps they prefer. Both groups dressed and danced in the instructor's style.

Conversely, I know an Atlanta troupe that dress and dance in a different style from their instructor. I've seen them do character dances, comedy routines, and storytelling dances. I've also seen them dance in unison and in matching costumes. Their instructor told me that she does not want to produce "clones" of herself on the stage.

She observed that some instructors produce performing troupes of dancers who are look-alikes of their teacher/choreographer; they dance her style and dress in a similar fashion. Some like this approach, while others do not. Either approach is fine, and it's up to you and your group to decide what you want to do.

Group improvisation

In a traditional example of a group improvisation, a troupe stands together. Taking turns, each dancer does a brief solo, while the supporting chorus of dancers is clapping and looking on from the background, or is mirroring her movements.

The popular American Tribal style of belly dance uses group improvisation extensively, using cues to communicate among dancers in the group. This style involves a group (tribe) of dancers following a lead dancer, and then rotating the leader. The lead dancer uses agreed-upon gestures and signals to alert the group to upcoming changes in the steps.

There are many other examples and styles of improvisation. It is interesting to begin a show by having many individual dancers weave their way through the audience, improvising to a piece of music. Then they can regroup on the stage and perform a choreography together.

A *collage* dance (called a *round robin* when performed by a group) may be performed on stage or as a class exercise. (Chapter 7 described methods for use with a soloist or group.) Round robin dances are useful for all levels of dancers, but are particularly good for beginners and for those who want to perform but feel less than comfortable doing a long solo.

In a round robin dance, each dancer takes turns performing as a soloist on the stage, but she only dances for about a minute, then leaves the stage as the next dancer comes on the stage. Depending on the length of the song, each dancer may have the opportunity to be on the stage more than once. A group of several dancers may "share" a solo in this way.

Random

Random or *chance dance* is useful as a group exercise in a classroom setting. It is different from improvising, and is essentially brief, sequential solos. Movements are randomly chosen, versus the spontaneous selection of movements inspired by hearing the music. This is a fun practice exercise for classes, to help students recall and remember the new movements they've learned.

An example of a random dance would be to write the names of various dance movements (or draw geometric patterns) on 3x5 note cards. Each student picks a card at random. Each dancer, in turn, shows the movement written on her card. (With the geometric pattern cards, each dancer selects the part of the body she uses to "draw" the pattern. Or, the geometric patterns may be useful as floor designs for traveling steps.)

Ripple

A *ripple* (also known as a *canon* or *fugue*) is a series of brief, identical and sequential solos. Dancers do a step (or a series of steps) in an identical sequence, performed by sequential dancers. It is useful in group belly dance routines as a bridge between segments of a choreography or improvised dance. While a ripple is usually a small portion of a dance routine, it is useful as a technique to create an entire dance in some situations.

The jazz "kick line" is a familiar example of a situation where ripples are used. A line of dancers is standing together, and the first dancer kicks her leg high, then the dancer standing beside her kicks, and on down to the end of the line, creating a "wave" or "ripple" effect.

In belly dance, any single step or any combination of steps may be used to start the ripple. (Examples: a single undulation, performed by sequential dancers, or an 8-count combination of steps performed by sequential dancers.)

"Random dance" design ideas to use in class exercises with cards. These designs may be used for hand, hip, shoulder movements or floor patterns.

Hilary Thacker (center) and her advanced student group in the U.K. Traveling steps and floor patterns result in different facing directions for individuals within a group. All the dancers are doing the same step, yet each photographs differently, creating a lovely picture.

Beginners through advanced levels dancing together

If you have a group with skill levels ranging from beginner to advanced, there are options for having them dance together on the stage. One possibility would be to choreograph a beginner segment of the dance, then an intermediate, then an advanced, having the dancers taking turns in groups (round robin style). Those waiting could stand behind the performing group, clapping, playing cymbals, or doing a simple line dance.

Another option is having the advanced group do all the performing on the stage, with the beginners being the back-up dancers and cymbal players throughout the performance, standing behind the main performers. This gives your entire group a chance to be shown to their best advantage; beginners get stage experience without too much pressure of performance, and intermediates and advanced levels get to show off their skills.

After the show is over

Dancers deserve praise and applause for giving a performance in front of an audience. Many people rank public speaking and public performance as their number one stressful situations, so being the focus of attention in public is a big accomplishment and worthy of recognition.

If you are a troupe director, make sure you give positive feedback to your group after the

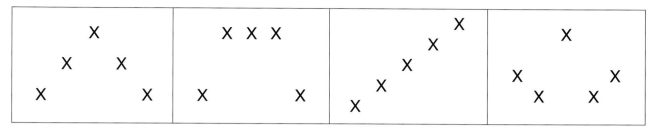

Floor pattern examples for a group of five dancers. Dancers transition between floor patterns with traveling steps. From left: dancers moving in unison, with a leader in front; a trio featured, background dancers moving in unison; a formation for a ripple; a soloist in front, with background dancers moving in unison.

show is over. Concentrate on the positive aspects of their performance. Mistakes happen and sometimes things don't come out perfectly, but in the overall scheme of things, audiences don't remember minor details very much.

One of my teachers gave her soloists and troupes small floral bouquets after performances, particularly after beginner students made their performing debuts. This was a nice gesture that made dancers feel appreciated.

Exercises:

Round robin for a group: Select a piece of music suitable for a *round robin*. How does the music cue the dancers that it's time for moving to the next soloist? How many changes of dance soloists does the music allow? Would it be easy to dance ad lib to this music? Is it easy for dancers to hear the musical changes in this song? *Variation:* using the same music, individual dancers act out a different character or theme for each change.

Random: Write down movements or movement combinations on note cards, then shuffle the cards

and take a few (3 or 4) from the deck. Dance these movements, putting them into a connected sequence (combination).

Ripple: Select a step or combination of steps. Dancer #1 does the step or combo, then Dancer #2 repeats, and on down the line. How would you adjust the step to fit your selected music? Steps can be big, small, fast or slow, and with pauses for emphasis which fit the music.

Troupe style: While watching a DVD or live troupe performance, observe how they organize their dance. Is it a "big solo" with everyone dancing in unison, or a series of sequential solos, or with dancers each performing different roles, or a mix of styles?

Troupe dance: Collaborating with a group or as part of a duet, experiment with improvisation, big solos and different roles. Find out what the members of your group enjoy most, and emphasize those qualities in your dance. Select a theme, scenario or storyline, motifs and music (see Chapter 5 for examples).

PART THREE

PRESENTATION SKILLS

OPPOSITE: *Asymmetrical poses are glamorous and effective on stage. Many poses in classical art are asymmetrical. Photo of Coco courtesy of the artist.*

CHAPTER NINE

Tips for Successful Performances

*"The most beautiful experience we can have is the mysterious.
It is the fundamental emotion that stands at the
cradle of true art and true science."*

ALBERT EINSTEIN (1879–1955)

*H*ave you seen a spectacular performance that left you in a state of enchantment? What made that performance stand out from others in your mind? It seems there is something mysterious or indefinable about spectacular performances.

Happily, there is common ground for great performances. Just as a well-written novel has a clearly defined beginning, middle, climax and ending, great dances contain certain elements that make them spectacular. Here are some tips and hints to help your dances be fun and successful:

Enjoy yourself

Enjoy yourself when you're dancing. If you're enjoying yourself, the audience will pick up on this feeling and have a good time too. However, everyone has good days and bad days. Professionals have to be prepared to look their best, even when having a bad day.

Also, a little tension is good. A Canadian dancer told me that she has so much experience performing that she rarely gets nervous anymore. Being in front of an audience has become commonplace for her. However, when she was invited to perform at a major international dance convention in front of many of her peers, she found herself in a more stress-inducing environment than her usual venues. She found that the increased tension gave her an extra boost of energy, which made her performance there truly outstanding.

Too much tension is detrimental. Stage fright is rooted in "what will they think of me?" It helps to focus on your dance rather than on what the audience

OPPOSITE: *A dance pose and a beautiful smile by Mahira. (The white background is the negative space in this photo.)*

may think. Having a strong, well-rehearsed beginning and ending to your dance is also a confidence-builder.

Leave them wanting more

"Leave them [the audience] *wanting more"* is a recurring theme in show business. Along the same lines, Doris Humphrey (a modern dance pioneer and choreographer) once declared, *"All dances are too long."*

Again, dance is like language. When giving a speech, after you've said what you need to say, it's time to summarize, wrap up, and depart the podium. I've sat in business meetings where discussions wandered into endless rambling. As entertainers, we want to avoid episodes of rambling on the stage at formal performances.

On the other hand, restaurant owners who hire dancers often want them to perform for extended periods. When working at a restaurant, paid performance, or formal stage presentation, make sure you have an agreement with your client/sponsor about how long they want you to dance. In most situations, it's best to get this in writing.

One of my teachers was surprised when a group featuring her in a large, well-publicized workshop asked her to limit her dance to only three minutes during the evening concert. She was also placed in the middle of the show, although she was the featured performer. This was extremely unusual, but it's what the sponsor wanted, and both parties agreed to this in advance. The dancer received the same pay as if she'd danced the usual twenty minutes.

Beautiful poses using positive and negative space

Positive and negative space is a design concept used frequently by sculptors, painters and artists, and also by choreographers. Good use of positive and negative space makes dance poses strong and defined.

There are two ways of drawing a subject (for example, an apple). You can either draw the apple itself (positive space), or draw the shape of the air surrounding the apple (negative space). If you draw the shape of the air surrounding the apple, you still end with an outline of an apple.

In dances, poses which take up lots of positive space express different feelings than poses which take up less space. For example, while looking in a mirror, hold your arms at your sides, elbows close to the body. There is no negative space between the arms and the torso. Next, pull your elbows away from the body. A negative triangular space is created between the arms and the torso. Which pose looks like a dance pose? The one with negative (background) space visible between the arms and the torso, because you (the "positive" image) take up more width. This pose looks "bigger" (see photo on page 88).

By being aware of your use of negative space, your use of positive space will also become stronger. Notice that many dance poses create interesting geometric patterns in the negative space (background). Dance instructors use the idea of negative space to help students use their arms effectively when they give cues such as, *"your arms should look as if you are holding a beach ball."* In other words, create a big, round negative space between the arms.

You can make your dances and your stage presence "bigger" by using space effectively. "Closed" movements and poses with less use of the surrounding negative space may be used to create stylized or classic designs, a meditative, inward-focused or introspective impression, or a pedestrian feeling. The impression also depends on the posture and facial expression that accompany the pose.

"Open" movements and poses use more space and create an outward-focused impression, such as an outgoing, friendly, happy or spacious feeling. The impression is also influenced by the dancer's posture and facial expression.

Both types of movement are expressive. Closed movements may gradually open to reflect an increase in intensity of the music, or a change in feeling from introspective to extroverted.

Symmetry and asymmetry

Using both asymmetry and symmetry gives a balanced look to dances. Asymmetrical lines are very important in visual art. A principle of photography is to show subjects off-center to present a more pleasing picture. Examples are abundant in advertising, newspaper, and glamour photography. Also, many poses in Persian miniature paintings and other classical art are based on asymmetry.

Symmetrical poses may be adapted into asymmetrical lines by using slight variations. For example, while shoulder shimmies are generally taught

with the arms held straight out from the body in a "T" position (as shown in the photo), tilting the arms adapts this into an asymmetrical "/" position. I remember a choreography taught by Ibrahim Farrah in which shoulder shimmies were done with the arms in a variety of angled positions. This enhanced the folkloric-style appearance of the movements.

Consider using asymmetrical floor patterns for variety. Asymmetrical floor patterns help hold the audience's attention, because they cannot predict what is coming next in the dance. Years ago, I watched a video of myself performing with a troupe in a dance involving a series of complicated steps forming a square floor pattern. Our group first drew the front of the square, then the right, then the rear, and then . . . you know what happens next. If this step sequence had been

Ramona greeting the audience with open arms; an open pose with symmetrical arm positions.

From left: symmetrical and asymmetrical floor pattern designs.

asymmetrical (such as by using a triangular or curving floor pattern instead of a square), it would have been less predictable.

On the other hand, symmetry in dance is also important. Symmetrical poses, floor patterns and movements definitely have their place. One of my teachers said that an audience member reminded her that she needed to remember to spin in both directions, not just in one direction, because she looked unbalanced.

Certain challenging movements are impressive to audiences when they are done on the right side of the body, then repeated on the left side of the body, because it shows that the dancer can do the movement on both sides. Symmetrical poses have a harmonious, balancing effect. Use both symmetry and asymmetry for variety.

Exercises:

Mental rehearsal of a successful performance: Close your eyes, begin music, visualize your performance

exactly the way you would like it to happen. Imagine the details: your hairstyle, costume, props, all being exactly the way you'd like them to be. In this relaxed state, rehearse your dance.

Personal enjoyment: Do you usually enjoy yourself when performing? Are you relaxed? If not, do you have ideas about how to make your performances more fun and less stressful? Having a pre-performance routine can reduce stress and remind you to relax. Some dancers meditate or take a few deep breaths, do a special warm-up exercise backstage, use a special perfume, aromatherapy, or another method to induce a feeling of well-being before performing on stage.

Many dancers find that having their costume ready and makeup done early reduces stress, while others work better under pressure and short time frames. This is a personal preference, find out what works best for you.

Positive and negative space: Look at the pictures in this book, and later notice photographs in newspapers and magazines. Focus on the background of the pictures, noticing the shapes which appear in the negative spaces. While improvising a dance, focus on the shapes in the negative space (for example, the space between the arms and torso). Using a mirror, notice the effect that this has on your gestures and movements.

Open and closed poses: While looking in a mirror, experiment with open and closed poses and dance movements. Notice how they look and feel. Do you usually find that one style of posing dominates your dancing, or do you use both open and closed poses equally? When you watch dance performances or attend classes, pay attention to how open and closed poses are used, and the feelings and impressions they express.

Asymmetrical floor patterns: Select a simple step pattern. (Example: step, touch or step, hop.) How would you make it asymmetrical? Experiment by using one traveling step and floor pattern to go to your destination, and a different step to return to your original location. Observe how this feels, and how it looks in a mirror.

Symmetry: Repeat the previous exercise, substituting symmetrical dance movements. Observe how this feels different from the previous exercise.

Floor pattern maps: Use pencil and paper to draw a doodle. Draw some curving lines, or an interesting pattern of straight lines. Or, draw a map or write your name. Dance this as a floor pattern.

Asymmetry: Select a combination of steps or a choreography you already know. Experiment by adding asymmetrical elements, while maintaining enough repetition so that the dance is easy to remember. (Example: instead of holding arms horizontally while doing a shoulder shimmy, tilt them sideways.)

Floor patterns and motifs: What floor pattern do you use most for traveling steps? (Popular examples are circles, L-shapes, and figure 8 motifs.) Experiment with a floor pattern that is new for you. (Ideas include geometric shapes such as triangles, diamonds, stars, and rectangles. Also, experiment with irregular shapes such as wavy lines.) A change of floor pattern may create an interesting variation in the feeling and appearance of your favorite step. Dance your favorite traveling steps in varying patterns. Observe how these variations feel, and how they look in a mirror.

CHAPTER TEN

Dance, Emotion and Expression

A dance expresses a lifetime in a moment.

*D*ance is an outward expression of a chain of events in our lifetime. A dance shows movements learned from our teachers, and the quality and frequency of our practice sessions. The art of dance is also a nonverbal language of the body, and expresses feelings and ideas that are outside the limits of spoken language. A dance also shows our personality, emotions, and inner soul, if we choose to *"let go," "be in the moment,"* and show it.

Dance as therapy

Dancing is therapeutic for many people. There is a branch of psychology called Dance/Movement Therapy (DMT) which helps people use body movement to gain access to their feelings to promote emotional healing. Our society places such emphasis on verbal communication that, unintentionally, we have distanced ourselves from our physical bodies. Society's emphasis is on communicating feelings and emotions with words and gestures alone, when sometimes these are inadequate.

Since not everyone is eloquent with language, dancing helps people express their feelings in a way that is more expressive for *them*. Before a child can make sentences, he or she can move to music. Dancing has a long history of expressing feelings, particularly happy feelings, without words. From millennia past and into the present day, dancing is linked with weddings and other joyful celebrations in both Eastern and Western civilizations, events where words are sometimes insufficient to express emotion. Dancing in the home is a part of daily life in some cultures.

The underlying mission of an instructor is not only to provide technical knowledge about dancing, but also to help students with expressing their feelings and their individuality through moving their bodies. Helping students discover their creative potential and express their individuality through movement gives both the student and the instructor an enormous sense of gratification.

To those who have a passion for dance, whatever their skill level, dance is therapeutic and life-enhancing. Joy is contagious to those who watch dancing and for those who dance.

Changing the motion changes the emotion. Ramona during a concert performance.

Changing the motion changes the emotion

There is a profound link between body movements, facial expressions, and emotions. Francois Delsarte said that *"motion creates emotion,"* and 50 years later the psychologist William James said that if you make movements expressive of joy, then you will feel joyous (and vice versa).

Researcher Paul Ekman observed that consciously changing your facial expression to a sad expression brings on feelings of sorrow, and changing to an angry expression brings on feelings of anger. This information is useful in therapy, but also applies to daily life. One of my friends "put on a happy face" to cope with the distress and anxiety of a frightening medical diagnosis and treatment program.

We can use this information in our daily lives. I've observed that when feeling fatigued, and then going out to teach a dance class or perform, after a few minutes into the dancing my energy level picks up. Dance movements that bring a smile to your face make you feel good inside too, and you communicate these feelings to the audience when you perform those movements for them.

While facial expressions influence feelings, dancers have noticed that certain body movements bring on particular feelings or emotions, and these are not necessarily the same for everyone. For example, when a group of dancers was discussing the hip shimmy, one remarked that it made her feel tired, while another dancer finds shimmies energizing and stimulating. A third dancer observed that the shimmy just feels like exercise to her. Another dancer said *"I go into a trance, and what happens is between me and God."*

Dance has a history of use as an informal method of therapy. Ibrahim Farrah remarked that the *Zar* ritual from Africa is useful for the "exorcism of a bad day." The Zar is a traditional way of releasing a "djinni" (genie), or spirits who are believed to cause distress, negativity and depression, especially to women.

The Zar traditionally consists of a group of women friends and relatives of the "patient," along with musicians and a female leader of the ritual. The ritual consists of specific rhythmic music and dance movements. The "patient" is guided through the *hadra* ritual by the leader, with the support of her friends, until exhausted.[27]

Scientists believe that the swinging movements of the body used in the Zar create chemical reactions in the body which alleviate depression. In any case, the movements of the Zar affect emotions and feelings; dancers report feeling extremely relaxed afterwards. Besides its traditional context, the Zar has also been staged as a performance piece. [28]

Releasing your inner dancer

While learning about dance technique, choreography, and music, the idea of *"surrendering to the moment"* and *"surrendering to the soul"* kept cropping up in literature and in discussions with dancers, choreographers, and musicians.

This idea goes further than being spontaneous; it means allowing the audience to "see into your soul" instead of doing "only" movements. The dancer is performing movements *for her personal satisfaction*, without being concerned about looking pretty or graceful. The dancer is not focusing on pleasing the audience. Instead, she is adopting a "letting it happen" versus a "making it happen" attitude toward dancing, with confidence that whatever happens during the dance will feel and look "right."

"Surrendering to the moment," or "letting go" is a very difficult thing for many of us. Modern work and office life consists of countless rules and prescribed behavior that make some of us live very scheduled, computerized and sometimes noncreative daytime lives. Dance classes provide a wonderful opportunity to socialize with others and reduce our stress level.

However, many dance classes focus on technique or choreographed dances which are very mechanical, intellectual exercises. These classes

teach us how to dance, but they don't teach us how to surrender to the moment, or how to relax into dance movements. A teacher can give guidance, but adopting a "letting it happen" attitude is something that advanced dance students must do for themselves.

Enhance your belly dance creativity

Creative expression lies in an area of deep concentration, combined with relaxation and inspiration. Artistic and athletic success depends on being relaxed and able to totally focus on the task at hand. Therefore, learning how to relax, "surrender," and "let go" can help you become more creative.

Many relaxation and concentration-enhancing techniques are available, including yoga asanas and breathing techniques, meditation, and dance meditation/improvisation. The Alexander Technique, which emphasizes optimal postural alignment, teaches body awareness, and recognition of physical areas holding tension, is particularly useful for dancers. All these methods focus on keeping your attention on what is happening in your body *right now*, instead of letting your mind wander.

Some dance teachers remind students to focus on the inward and outward flow of breath during challenging movements, to enhance the relaxation/creativity process. This technique helps us be "in the moment" and enhances expressiveness.

Birthing belly dance

Modern dance pioneer Doris Humphrey said *"There is only one thing to dance about: the meaning of one's personal experience."* A dance is the cumulative expression of a lifetime in a moment. A lifetime of experiences is expressed in dancing. Our posture and facial expressions show feelings; our move-

ments show our dance education and physical fitness level; our steps show the dance styles we've studied; our selection of music says something about our preferences and dance background. The way we put it together with choreography or improvisation shows something deeply personal about the way we experience dance and interpret music.

The experience of giving birth has connections with dance. Birth has been called *"the dance of life,"* and *"a lifetime in a moment."* Like a dance, the way a woman gives birth poignantly expresses her individuality, attitude toward life, and the essence of her personal belief system. The cumulative experiences and attitudes she's developed during her life, and the chain of events leading up to pregnancy and birth express her individuality. Professional childbirth assistants (doulas) have noted

Birthing a belly dance. Ramona dancing in her second trimester. (Photo by Tereza Gomes.)

OPPOSITE: *Ramona releasing her inner dancer. (Eye of the Beholder photography by Chris.)*

that a woman's personality is an important factor in how she gives birth.[29]

I have heard statements such as *"my dance comes from God,"* and many dancers refer to the spiritual, deeply stirring feelings that dance brings them. Some call it *"being in the moment," "living in present time"* or *"surrendering to the soul."* Some see dance as a spiritual journey. I was particularly touched by a story I heard about a woman in labor which expresses this idea:

> A woman arrived at a birthing center, apparently not in significant pain or distress, and calmly told the midwife that she was going to give birth very soon. The midwife did not believe her, because she was not behaving like a typical client in the late stages of labor. The woman was relaxed and serene. Therefore, the midwife was surprised when the woman easily gave birth a half hour later. The midwife had never before seen anyone who gave birth as easily as this woman, so she asked the client why she'd been so serene. The woman replied that her mother had told her what to expect during labor: *"You will feel God's power coming through you, and you should do everything possible to welcome it."*

Our life experiences, individuality, and beliefs profoundly affect not only how we dance and give birth, but also how we choose to live our lives. This is another outward expression of the pervasive link between mind and body. The woman in labor knew how to surrender to her soul when she needed to, and many dancers surrender to the soul during their performances.

Exercises:

Role model: Who is your favorite role model in dance? What characteristics make this dancer uniquely expressive? What is most memorable about a performance from this person? Inspiration from other dancers can be a springboard for developing your own creative ideas.

Dance as meditation: After a few minutes of meditation or deep breathing for relaxation, dance to music. Focus on maintaining a relaxed state. Afterwards, take a few minutes to write about the experience. Additional insights frequently come when writing.

Changing the motion/emotion: Rehearse to a familiar song, dancing various movements in your repertoire. Practice each movement long enough to observe whether it brings up any specific feelings. Does any particular movement always bring a smile to your face? Does a specific movement make you feel happy, tired, energized or sensual? What other feelings arise when you dance?

Relaxation: Improvise to a familiar song, and do not watch in the mirror. Next, improvise again, but watch yourself in the mirror this time. How did the two experiences feel? How do you think the mirror changed your dancing?

Art and feelings: Draw a picture of someone or something, or select an existing photo. The art could be a landscape, self-portrait, special pet or anything of significance to you. Then, dance the image. (Example: if the picture is composed of straight lines, use straight movements, for curved lines use curved movements. Or, just dance the way the image makes you feel. Example: a celebration picture evokes happy feelings, happy facial expression and energetic movements such as hops and kicks.)

How did you feel before and after your dance? Take a few minutes to write about the experience, since additional insights frequently come from writing.

CHAPTER ELEVEN

Designing a Bellydance Show

"A true leader always keeps an element of surprise up his sleeve, which others cannot grasp but which keeps his public excited and breathless."

CHARLES DE GAULLE (1890–1970)

*P*art of the role of dance instructors and is to show leadership by organizing performances. Most teaching artists are responsible for putting together shows or salons for their students, and sometimes are responsible for organizing bigger events as well. Venues often include concert performances, workshop shows, charity events and restaurant performances.

What is the best way to organize diverse acts or solo dances into a show? Composing a show is similar to composing a song, including these parts:

• *Introduction,* setting the mood, invoking excitement in the audience, giving a hint of things to come; in the

• *Middle* comes a variety of musical talent and dance innovation, expressing the joy, soulful expression and contemplative emotion of dance; and a memorable, climactic

• *Finale* sending the audience home with great memories, and leaving them wanting more.

Theme

There are many options for organizing a dance concert. The most basic is letting the performers select whatever they want to do, and then arranging the performances, alternating solo and group dances.

A storytelling show would also have an easy-to-organize format. For example, a theme show based on *"Belly dancing throughout the ages"* would start with an old-style dance (examples: Phaeronic, or other theme associated with antiquity), then different dances showing the evolution of dance throughout history. The finale might feature a soloist or troupe doing a futuristic or contemporary modern number. You could ask performers to select which segment of history they'd like to do, then organize the dances into this format.

The ideas for theme shows are unlimited!

Establishing good feelings

Warm-up music played at a reasonable volume is a nice touch before the show, to set the mood as the audience comes in to take their seats. A slide show of scenes related to the show's theme and accompanied by music is also a great way to entertain the audience and build interest prior to the beginning of a show.

It is good to start a show with a high-energy troupe number to get off to a strong start. Later, more serious or contemplative dances can be presented. If there is an intermission between acts, it is good to start the second half of the show with another high-energy troupe or solo number, to rebuild the excitement for the second act. Generally, a featured soloist or strong troupe performance ends the evening with a climactic dance.

Many dancers also appreciate the opportunity for open dancing and audience participation when the show is over, especially if there is a live band.

Introductions

The announcer/MC is important, and their comments should be brief. When there are lengthy introductions for each performer, this is tiring for the audience and causes the show to lose momentum. For example, in a show with 12 performers where each introduction takes four minutes, the audience ends up listening to 36 minutes of introductions. If there is a delay, such as the MC walking on and off the stage to get to a microphone, this takes even more time.

A program with photos and bios of each dancer tells the audience about each performer without having to announce details verbally. If this is done, usually all the performers are called back to the stage at the end of the show for recognition and a photo opportunity.

For shows with fewer performers, more time is taken with announcing, but comments should still not be too lengthy.

Also, I think it is good to give your dances titles, since it makes the dances more memorable. It is customary to name dances in ballet and other genres. The title should evoke an image of what the dance is about. One particularly memorable belly dance I saw was titled *"The Snake,"* and was performed by a soloist wearing a snake-print costume and featured slithering S-curving movements.

Organizing music

It is appropriate to begin a show with a happy, high-energy song to entertain and get the audience involved. A variety of dances follow. More "serious" musical pieces may also be presented. It is generally not appropriate to begin a dance concert with heart-wrenching music. Energy level and emotion must first be established. Think of a show as story, complete with a musical introduction, highlights, climactic points and finale.

Exercises:

Theme show: Imagine a show in which each dance relates to a central theme, and with variations on that theme. Some dances in your show could be serious, others comic or novelty.

- How would you narrate the show?
- Which dances would be appropriate for group performances? Soloists?
- What props would be needed to set the scenes?

OPPOSITE: *Accepting applause after a show. Performance styles featured in the show included Modern American, Modern Egyptian, Raqs Shamadan, and Tribal Fusion. Top row, from left: Ramona, Fereshteh Hosseini, Saroya. Front row: Oracle and Fatina.*

Example: a theme show about *"Belly dancing through history"* could include dances such as "Cave Woman," "Cleopatra," "Little Egypt" and "Modern American." Other ideas: *"Scenes from Cairo"* (various dance scenes including weddings, nightclubs, restaurants, parties); *"Dances of America,"* to include jazz, ballet, baton, ballroom, hip-hop, and belly dance performances (for a school which offers many forms of dance).

Establishing good feelings: Contemplate ways of establishing good feelings before the performance begins. (Example: What kind of background music would you use to set the mood? Would you have a "greeter" at the door of the theater to hand out programs?)

Introductions: Think of a creative and brief way to announce each performer. Examples:

- Drumroll, then the dancer's or troupe's name sung out by vocalist.
- Posterboards printed with the performer's name danced across the stage by a helper, youth, or costumed character.
- MC dressed in a costume announcing performer's names.
- What are your ideas?

PART FOUR

MUSIC AND DANCE

Experienced musicians focus their attention on the dancer, in order to synchronize their music with the dancer's movements. Photo of Halimeda and Mike courtesy of JAPHO Photography and Jeff Mischke.

CHAPTER TWELVE

Musical Finesse

*"Music… can name the unnameable and
communicate the unknowable."*

LEONARD BERNSTEIN (1918–1990), COMPOSER

Music can make or break a dance performance. Songs can move us deeply.
They may make us feel happy or sad, bring us into a state of prayer and meditation, make us feel like dancing or put us to sleep. It's important to select
appropriate music for belly dancing, since music has components of emotion
and language, just as conversations do.

There was a show many years ago where a dancer performed to a song in a
foreign language, and people in the audience responded by crying. The song
had a sorrowful theme about the destruction caused by war. Because the dancer
didn't speak their language, she had no idea why her dance caused this distressed reaction. This is an extreme example of why it is important to know
more about your music than whether it simply sounds nice.

This chapter includes information about actively listening to music, selecting
appropriate songs, using the rule of four, understanding rhythms, working with
musicians, musical nuances of dancing with percussive beats, and more!

Listening to music

There are different ways of listening to music:

- *Analytical*
- *Physical*
- *Emotional*
- *Passive*

When we listen to music in an *analytical* way, we identify or recognize something about the way the music is put together. You may recognize patterns
within the music, or count beats, or recognize different instruments, or you may
listen to the melody or the lyrics. You identify whether the song is from your
own culture or not, whether the vocalist is male or female, whether there is a
chorus, and other specifics of the way the song is presented.

When we listen to music in a *physical* way, we feel a physical reaction to the music somewhere in the body. Some songs cause our hearts to speed up, slow down, make us feel happy or relaxed, or we may feel a gut reaction, tap our feet intuitively, or find ourselves drifting off to sleep while listening to music.

When we listen to music *emotionally*, we respond to the music within our souls. Maybe there is a special song that you remember from a relationship with a loved one, or from your wedding, or a song which reminds you of an especially happy or sad time in your life. When you hear the song again, whatever the current circumstances, it brings back the feelings and memories from the past. You may be hearing the song for the first time or the fiftieth time, and somehow it brings up an emotion or memory.

Lastly, when listening to music in a *passive* way, such as subdued background music in a waiting room or other public place, we are aware of it, but not focused on it. We may choose to ignore it or tune it out of our consciousness. We hear it with the mechanics of the ear, but otherwise aren't responding to it; our minds are focused elsewhere.

Selecting music for your performance

There are many CDs produced specifically for belly dancing. Look for them in the international section of your local music store, or get them from belly dance suppliers. Most recordings labeled "belly dance" contain music recorded in the U.S., Near East or Asia Minor, and have lyrics sung in Arabic, Turkish or other languages.

Use recordings that have a photo of a belly dancer on the cover, or make sure you know the theme of the album (love songs, for example). Many foreign CDs now include translations of the titles of the songs, and many also include English translations of the lyrics. Song translations may sometimes be found with an Internet search engine, and the Shira.net website is a helpful

resource with more than 100 belly dance song translations. If the CD is not labeled as dance music, it is best to find out the general translation of the music. This is especially important if you plan on dancing with it in front of an audience.

Using music with lyrics sung in foreign languages can be problematic unless you are very familiar with the language and the culture. A dancer told me that she often used a particular song during years of performances, then later found that the lyrics translated as *"her house is like the airport; the men fly in and out."* If she had known the translation, she wouldn't have selected this song. Even if you're dancing with a singer and a live band, it's good to find out ahead of time what lyrics they plan to use.[30]

When I trained as a jazz dancer, my instructor told us not to use songs with vocals, because she said that singing takes the audience's attention away from the dancer. Belly dancers' opinions vary on this subject.

Instrumental versions of songs composed for the Egyptian singer Uum Kalthoum are classic choices for dance performances. Instrumental songs including *Alf leyla wa leyla* (1001 Nights), *Lisah faker* (Do you still remember?), *Fakkarouni* (They reminded me), *Ani fi intizarak* (I'm waiting for you) and many more appear on many belly dance CDs. Many of these songs have been updated and remixed to create a modern sound. Also, know that it is not appropriate to use recordings of Uum Kalthoum's voice for a dance performance, due to the unique standing of this beloved singer in Middle Eastern culture.[31]

Though most belly dance music is in the Near Eastern style, there are other options for musical accompaniments. Many dancers are now performing "fusion" pieces to worldbeat music. For example, some Latin American songs are popular for belly dancing. Successful dances have also been done to popular American music, and also music from other countries. Oriental dance has become quite popular in France, and many popular belly dance songs are now in the French language. Also, there are belly dance songs in Spanish, Russian, and other languages.

Lastly, the most important requirement for dance music is that it must inspire *you*!

Rule of four

Belly dance music contains repetitions of musical phrases or themes. When listening to music in an analytical way, you may hear a musical phrase repeated four times, and then the music changes; a different musical phrase, tempo, or instrument is introduced. The fourth repetition is the *transition* or *bridge* into the new musical phrase. The fourth repetition may be an exact repetition of previous phrases, or a variation.

Example:

- Drummer plays a basic slow chifte telli rhythm (8 counts)
- Repeat
- Repeat
- Embellished slow chifte telli *(bridge)*
- Change to fast maqsum rhythm *(tempo and rhythmic change)*

The *rule of four* is useful to dancers, because it lets us know when changes are coming up. We know that we can generally expect four sets of a musical phrase, or three sets with a transition. However, the Rule of four is not without a few exceptions, and there are some songs which don't follow this rule at all.

In general, a dancer may choose to repeat a selected movement pattern four times before changing to something new, and this follows along with the music. Dancers sometimes use three exact repetitions, followed by a "bridge" or variation of dance steps, and then start a new pattern.

Example of a dance combination, using the rule of four:

- Step-together-step with rib circles to the right
- Repeat
- Repeat
- Step-together-step with rib circles to the left *(bridge)*
- Undulation/camel in place *(new pattern)*

Rhythms

Drumbeats are the heartbeats of belly dance music. A dancer must be able to understand rhythm in order to dance well. It is critical that dancers aspiring to advanced or professional level performances know the basic rhythms in belly dance music. This also helps her with learning finger cymbal patterns.

The most commonly found rhythms in belly dance music are in 4/4 time, which musicians count as: "1 and 2 and 3 and 4 and," while dancers count 4/4 as: "1, 2, 3, 4, 5, 6, 7, 8." In general, rhythms in 4/4 time are easiest for beginners to dance to, since the vast majority of popular music in our culture is also in this familiar time signature. It is easier for mainstream American audiences to tap their feet and clap to the rhythm of 4/4 drumbeats.

Many rhythms used in belly dance music are in 4/4. Examples include *masmoudi sagheer* (small masmoudi), *Saiidi*, *slow chifte-telli*, *rumba*, and *bolero*. American audiences relate well to these rhythms because they have a familiar beat, yet also have a belly dance sound. Rhythms in 2/4, including *fallahi* and *ayuub*, are also popular with dancers and audiences; 2/4 is found in both slow trance music and in upbeat dance music.

OPPOSITE: *Egyptian baladi dance performance by Hilary Thacker in Edinburgh, Scotland. Hilary is wearing her antique Egyptian red assuit costume. Tiny silver bars are pressed into mesh fabric to create assuit. Rare white assuit can be colorfully dyed, while black is the typical color.*

Baladi (also spelled *beledi* or *balady*) is an Egyptian term which refers to folkloric and traditional Egyptian styling. It refers to a traditional lifestyle and to a folkloric dance style. "Baladi dance" refers to traditional Egyptian dance with music which is lively and fun. In America, dancers refer to the *masmoudi sagheer* rhythm (also called *maksoum*) as *baladi*.[32]

Dance music in 8/4 and 10/4, such as *masmoudi karir* (big masmoudi) (8/4) and *samai* (10/4) are slower in tempo. Turkish and Greek belly dance music use the familiar 4/4 time signature, but also have music counted in 5, 7, and 9 beat patterns (5/8, 7/8, 9/8). *Karsilama* is the fast 9/8 which is popular for high-energy Turkish dances. These time signatures sound exotic to some audiences, because the time signatures and rhythms are not found in American pop music.

A qualified dance or percussion instructor can help you with counting music and learning Near Eastern rhythms. (The Resources section also lists helpful DVDs, CDs and books.)

Dance styles and rhythms

Some rhythms have traditional styling and particular steps which go along with them. For example, belly dance teachers versed in Turkish dance train their students to use steps which accompany the 9/8 rhythm, and in using Turkish Roman (also called *Rom, Roma*) steps and gestures to accompany the karsilama rhythm. *Persian 6/8, Saiidi* (Upper/Southern Egyptian) and *kahliji* (also spelled *kaleegi*, a rhythm from the Gulf) call for particular styling and movements.

Sometimes the music style dictates the type of dance and costume that are appropriate. Also, some traditional costumes call for a certain sort of movement, since the range of motion affects the steps a dancer can do while wearing the garment.

Segments of khaliji music within belly dance songs call for kahliji movements. Oracle demonstrates a hair toss. (Photo courtesy of Dance of the Fates.)

It is a joy to dance with professional musicians. Hilary Thacker dancing with professional Egyptian nai and darbuka musicians in the U.K.

For example, women's kahliji dances are performed wearing *thobes* (very long, embroidered caftan-like overdresses with very wide sleeves). The most universally recognized women's dance movement of this style is the "dance of the hair" (*raqs na'shaar* or *raks al nasha'at*), where the hair swings from side to side in an arc. The embroidery on the thobe is showcased by the dancer holding the thobe while taking small steps.

Segments of folkloric music are included in some Oriental belly dance songs; a dancer may use folkloric movements during those segments to go along with that feeling.

Dancing with live bands

When dancing with musicians in a live performance, talk to them in advance about the kind of music they will play for you. Learn *their* language; some musicians ask you to specify fast or slow tempos, while other musicians are open to being asked for specific rhythms or songs. (Example of a music request: a medium tempo song to start, a taqsim, then a fast-paced drum solo to finish the set.)

Musicians do not understand what a dancer wants when she tells them a specific movement she wants to do, and then expects the musician to select and play a song to accompany her. A musician gave me this example, from a conversation with a dancer before a show: *"I want to open with a veil, then do a spin, a shimmy, and then . . ."* The musician said he had absolutely no idea what music the dancer wanted, based on this description. Listing movements generally doesn't make sense to musicians, because it is not their language. They understand tempo, rhythms and names of songs.

Another musician commented that it is annoying to be playing for a dancer when she is not listening to him. Again, dance is like communication; when dancing with live music (or recorded music, for that matter), the "conversation" taking place is between the dancer, the musician(s) and the audience. The music and the dance need to merge, and in order for that to happen, everyone onstage needs to be aware of what the others are doing.

Variations in dancing with the drumbeat

Professional musicians keep their attention on the dancers they are playing for, in order to synchronize their music with the dancer's movements. Dancers and musicians who frequently work together establish a working relationship where they communicate very well with each other onstage.

Professional dancers communicate onstage with musicians by using gestures to speed up, slow down, wind it up, and so on. One of the professional musicians I worked with asked me to do a series of spins to let him know when I was ready to end a dance.

Much of the communication is nonverbal, and the way the dancer moves to drumbeats is another way she communicates with her musicians during live performances. Being aware of the beat of the music is very important. In general:

- Dancing ahead of the beat expresses enthusiasm, lots of energy, anticipation, and the feeling that the dancer is leading the music (or that the dancer left out steps or is rushing).

- Being exactly on the beat connotes precision, power and confidence (or that the dancer is counting every beat).

- Dancing behind the beat, or "almost late" gives the impression that the music is propelling the dancer forward, and that the dancer is listening to and spontaneously responding to the music (or that the dancer doesn't know the music or the choreography).

Much of what is communicated by the dancer is open to interpretation. The dancer's facial expression and use of the body shows the audience that she's precisely on the beat because she knows the music very well, or that she's precisely on the beat because her facial expression shows intense concentration on counting. This is an area where the experience and skill of the dancer comes into play. Being ahead of, on, or after the beat is ideally the dancer's choice, rather than happening randomly.

Being ahead of, on, or after the beat expresses different feelings, depending on the dancer's preference. For example, being on the beat may communicate robot-like precision or express powerful and passionate emotion, *depending on the context.* The context is all the other expressive details of the dance: the thoughts in the dancer's mind that influence her posture, facial expression, gestures, and movements.

Most dancers like to be exactly on the beat. However, dancing a split second ahead of or behind the beat is a technique useful at times with a live band, because the dancer is giving the band a cue with her movements. When she dances slightly ahead of the music, she is nonverbally asking the band to speed up, and when she stops to end the dance she is telling the band to stop. Thus, she is leading the musicians with her movements.

On the other hand, being ahead of the beat with recorded music may show the audience that the dancer doesn't know her choreography or music and is rushing though the song. (Need help finding the beat? See *"Touch training tip"* in Chapter 14.)

Here is an example of using the beat:

A drumming student told me that he does not watch the dancer he is playing for, because it is too distracting for him to concentrate on the dancer and his drumming at the same time. I was to dance at a festival while he played the drum for me. I decided to dance behind the beat ("almost late," a split second behind the beat) so that his music propelled me through the dance. I needed to have time to hear his music, interpret it and respond to it with my movements. It was not appropriate to dance ahead of the beat (since he was not watching me for cues), and I couldn't dance exactly on the beat because I didn't know what was coming next in his improvisation. Our performance together was a lot of fun, and was well-received by the audience.

This example shows why it is so important to talk with your musicians ahead of time, so that you may know what to expect and be prepared. It is a real joy to dance with professional musicians, not only because of the quality of their music, but also because they make a dancer's job easier.

Most of the time, dancers improvise movements when working with live bands. However, I saw one troupe that danced choreography with their live band. If you choose to do this, it's a good idea to have a back-up plan if some part of the music gets changed inadvertently. The troupe I saw was thrown off their choreography when the live band added extra counts into the middle of the song, but they handled it well, and the audience didn't notice.

Finally, it is important to acknowledge the musicians either before or after the performance. Introduce the members of the band individually, so they may take a bow and accept applause.

Dancing to your own beat

Self-accompaniment is a method of adding the excitement of live music to your group or solo performances without hiring a band, and without recorded music. I've seen a impressive troupe and solo performances where dancers accompanied themselves with finger cymbals (known in Arabic as *sagat*, in Turkish as *zils*) while dancing.[33] They played cymbals throughout the song, with no other musical accompaniment.

Other ideas for self-accompaniment are fun too. Jamila Salimpour used to perform a percussion solo by coordinating the sounds of her coin belt with the sounds of her cymbals.[34] Some troupes accompany themselves on the darbuka (Near Eastern goblet-shaped drum) while dancing.

If you want to accompany yourself with your own music, such as drum, tambourine, or cymbals, be certain that your counting is even. Practice with CDs, and use an audio or video recorder. A metronome (timing device available at music stores) is also helpful. Play back your recorded practice to find out where you need to make changes. Get coaching from an instructor who has mastered your instrument, if possible.

A tip for keeping time during drum solos is having a tambourine or other instrument repeating a simple rhythm in the background. This helps the drummer find the background rhythm after they finish their solo, and it helps the dancer and the band stay on the beat as well. Also, be aware that:

- Self-accompaniment, particularly with troupe dances, requires music which is *simple and repetitive*, unless the dancers are also advanced-level musicians. It is difficult to do anything other than basic rhythms while dividing concentration between dance steps and playing a

musical instrument (this includes playing finger cymbals).

- Because the music is simple and repetitive for self-accompanied dances, make sure the dance is not too long. Remember the show business adage *"Leave them wanting more,"* particularly when performing self-accompanied dances.

- *"When you play cymbals, you are a member of the band,"* is something my teacher Kalila emphasized. Use an audio or video recorder while you're practicing playing finger cymbals. Play the recording and listen. In this way, you can easily identify and correct your mistakes before getting in front of an audience. Using a recorder and listening to your practice sessions will improve your cymbal playing enormously!

How to improve your understanding of music, guaranteed!

Learn to play an instrument. This will improve your musicality enormously, and there is no substitute for it. If there are no instructors in your area, get instructional materials and spend the time to learn it yourself at home. It takes time and practice, but it works. Here are some ideas:

- Books, tapes, DVDs and CDs covering finger cymbal, darbuka, tambourine, tar and muzhar technique are available via mail order (see Resources). Learning to play any of these instruments will enhance your understanding of Near Eastern music, which will enhance your dance performances.[35] Some restaurants require that their belly dance performers play finger cymbals, so having this skill may influence how much work they offer a dancer.

OPPOSITE: *Dancing with a tambourine is fun and easy. Photo of Saroya of Atlanta courtesy of the artist.*

- Do you like to sing? Remember that your voice is a musical instrument. If you enjoy singing and want to learn more about it, consider taking voice lessons or joining a choral group. This will also improve your skills and enhance your musical understanding. Interestingly, it used to be customary for dancers in Egypt and other parts of the Near East to be singers as well (this is not so in the present day). The two arts call upon similar skills with respect to understanding music.

Music takes place in fractions of time. The written language of music is in fractions (2/4, 4/4, 5/8, 8/4, 10/4, etc.). Musicians keep track of these fragments of time and keep them organized. Thankfully, we don't have to be good mathematicians to be good at playing music. If you can count from one through eight, you can learn to play percussion. As an added benefit, playing an instrument is a great source of relaxation and stress relief.

When I was in school, music was always one of my worst subjects. I played the flute very poorly for many years in the school band. Later, learning to play cymbals was a frustrating challenge. However, I really wanted to learn to play them, and so I persisted. It took some lessons with a great teacher and more time-consuming home practice, which worked!

I thought I was a hopeless musician. However, with good training and practice, today I believe there is hope for *everyone*, if the student has the desire and the stick-to-it-ness to put forth the effort. A patient and understanding teacher who gives clear directions is very important.

The key is to find an instrument that you like. One reason I was such a terrible flute player was that I never thought that the songs I was required to play in the band were very exciting to listen to. Find an instrument that excites your imagination and that you enjoy hearing, then get help learning how to play it.

Be aware that the better you become at playing the instrument of your choice, the more you enjoy it. Then you get even better at playing it, then you learn more, enjoy your instrument even more, become even better at playing, and the cycle continues.

Practice and knowledge make perfect

This chapter touches briefly on the basics of understanding musical composition. Much more information is available about musical notation, composition, music therapy and other related topics. See the Resources section for books and instructional recordings on the subject. Listening to and dancing with a variety of music will also increase your understanding.

Exercises:

Physical listening: Sit or lie down in a comfortable position. With eyes closed, listening to the music, focus on where in your body you feel physical responses. Listen again while standing with eyes open, improvising movements based on where you feel physical responses.

Emotional listening: Before listening to a song, notice your current state of mind and mood. Listen to a song, improvising dance movements, and afterwards notice how you felt during and after the song played. How did the music and movement affect your mood or feelings? Do some songs affect you differently from others? If so, how?

Analytical listening and the rule of four: Listen to any belly dance song, noticing the musical phrasing. Do you hear the same musical phrase four times, and then hear a new musical phrase? Are the changes obvious or subtle in the music you selected?

Beats: During your next practice, notice your habits with using music. Identify the beat by tapping your foot in time with the drumbeats, or by clapping your hands. (See Chapter 14, *"Touch training tip"* if you are having difficulty identifying the beat.) When dancing with the music, are you usually moving ahead of the beat, on the beat, "almost late" or behind the beat? Experiment with moving with the beat in different ways, and notice how each variation feels.

Dancing to your own rhythm: Select an instrument (or clap your hands), and play a rhythmic pattern to accompany an improvised dance during your next practice session. Afterwards, practice dancing again with your instrument or hand-clapping, this time improvising to recorded music. Compare how the two experiences felt, and notice what you learned about music from the experience.

Selection of Near Eastern instruments against an assuit fabric backdrop. From left: a frame drum, Egyptian mizmar and darbuka, and a Turkish oud. The darbuka shown is a traditional style, with inlaid shell designs and a fish skin drum head. (Photo courtesy of Hilary's Bazaar.)

CHAPTER THIRTEEN

Musical Patterns in Your Favorite Songs

"Music is well said to be the speech of angels."

THOMAS CARLYLE (1795–1881), HISTORIAN AND ESSAYIST

Great music combined with a talented dancer has the power to move us deeply, just as well-chosen words combined with a good speaker have the power to move us deeply. Music is like a conversation or a speech.

Just as a person greets a new acquaintance with, *"Hello, I'm (name),"* a song also has an introduction, then moves into a conversation between different instruments. After the intro, the "conversation" gets going and gains momentum. There are highlights and climactic points in music, and then the song comes to a conclusion, the *"good-bye"* that ends the conversation. Although a dancer may wait in the wings or walk onto the stage during the introduction, the bigger, more powerful dance movements usually start when the "conversation" begins, and *not* with the introduction. Listen for a change in the instrumentation or tempo to identify the starting point of the conversational part of the music.

Just as there are different types of conversations, such as a speech by one person or a complex discussion between many people, songs also have different formats. For example, drum solos have a different feeling than songs played by an orchestra, and singers add yet another dimension. After the introduction, songs show their format.

Let's explore the different elements of songs, recognizing that songs may contain one, two or more of these. Some of the following terms will be familiar to you from the discussion of formatting dances in Chapter 7, but in this chapter they are applied to music:

- *Taqsim*
- *Binary (AB)*
- *Ternary (ABA)*
- *Verse and chorus*
- *Rondo*
- *Theme and variations*
- *Suite*

OPPOSITE: *Taqsim instrumentals (see next page) are popular choices for sword dances due to the taqsim's slow tempo. Coco shows an American cabaret style approach to dancing with a sword.*

Taqsim

A *taqsim* (pronounced "talk-seem," also spelled *taxim,* plural: *taqaseem*) is an improvisational piece of instrumental Near Eastern music, with or without a rhythmic drumbeat, and usually with a slow tempo. The slow *chifte telli* rhythm, and other metric and non-metric patterns, are used for taqaseem.

Belly dancers generally use this part of the music to show their skill with slow, contemplative movements and improvisational skills; they express sensuous feelings. Due to the slow tempo of a taqsim, movements are introverted rather than extroverted, with a feeling of seriousness or reflectiveness; a taqsim is hypnotic, mesmerizing and meditative.

Slow dance movements convey serious, profound emotions, sensuality, or a regal, majestic feeling, reflecting the long, slow musical phrases in a taqsim. Notice the long, sustained breaths of the wind instruments in a taqsim, and that long, slow dance movements mirror this pattern of breathing.

Deep breathing is associated with great effort and profound emotions. The long, extended breaths of the wind instruments in some taqaseem evoke movements that reflect these serious feelings, such as slow undulations, belly rolls and hip movements that involve the dancer using a pattern of slow, deep breathing. These movements express emotion coming from the soul, going into the torso, then into the face, arms, hands, legs and then communicated outward to the audience.

A taqsim may be an entire song on a CD, or a section within a song. Some belly dance songs begin with a brief introductory taqsim, followed by an upbeat song. (Before the technology of recorded music, *taqaseem* used to be a long part of some live musical performances.)

A taqsim may be played by many different instruments. Some favorites are *oud* (lute), *ney* (Near Eastern reed flute), *drum* and *violin.* But you may also hear slow improvisational music played by other instruments such as the *electric guitar, accordion, saxophone, clarinet* and *buzuq* (long-necked lute).

Binary (AB format)

Binary format is a section A followed by a contrasting section B. One way to identify changes in the music is to listen for differences in instrumentation. For example, the first part of an AB format song may be all string instruments with a flowing feeling (segment A), then a contrasting percussive drum solo (segment B) which ends the song.

This format is almost never used in songs, but I often see workshop performances in this format.

Example:

A: Dancer begins with a dance to an Egyptian pop song.
B: Dancer ends performance with a drum solo *(music and feeling contrast A).*

Ternary (ABA format)

Ternary format, called "ABA," is much more common in songs than Binary format. ABA appeals to listeners because the repeat of segment A gives the song a well-rounded feeling. The listener gets a nice "know what's going to happen" feeling near the conclusion of the song, due to the repeating segment at the end. Ternary belly dance music is usually at a moderate or upbeat tempo, conveying an extroverted, energetic feeling.

A song in ternary format contains:

A: *Statement* of one or more musical themes.
B: *Variation* of those themes (or introduction of new and different themes).
A: *Restatement,* where the original theme is repeated (perhaps with variations).

Example:

A: Vocalist sings a verse with the accompaniment of the whole band *(theme)*.
B: Drum solo *(bridge; a new theme)*.
A: Vocalist reprises the verse with the accompaniment of the band, song ends *(theme)*.

Transitional phrases are short (usually a few bars of music) between the segments, and help the song flow. Contrasting Section B acts as a *bridge* between segments.

Verse and chorus

Many belly dance songs are organized in the *verse and chorus* format (also called *question and answer, call and response,* or *call and reply,* because it sounds conversational).[36] It consists of verses, either sung or instrumental, alternating with a chorus, and organized in a repeating sequence. The tempo of these belly dance songs is at a moderate or upbeat tempo, conveying a more extroverted feeling than the slow, instrumental taqsim.

Many popular songs are arranged in the verse and chorus format; listen to your radio and you'll hear examples of verse and chorus format in American pop music, church music, children's songs and classical music.

Verse and chorus in belly dance music does not necessarily mean that singing is involved. Instrumental songs in this format are on many belly dance CDs, including some drum solos.

Example:

A: Melody played by entire band *(verse)*
B: Percussion solo *(chorus)*
A: Melody with variations by entire band *(verse)*
B: Percussion solo *(chorus)*
A: Melody with variations by entire band, ending the song *(verse)*

Rondo

The *rondo* is a common format in belly dance music, and is a variation of the verse and chorus, but with added variety. Like the verse and chorus, a rondo in belly dance music is usually at a moderate or upbeat tempo, conveying an extroverted, energetic feeling.

What is rondo? If you called a verse "A" and a chorus "B," in rondo these musical segments (perhaps with variations) repeat themselves throughout the song. However, between these repeating segments are other contrasting segments (let's call these "C," "D," etc.).

Example:

* Verse, chorus, and another verse ("ABA"),
* Contrasting segment (example, accordion solo "C")
* Repeat of verse "A"
* Another contrasting segment (example, clarinet solo "D")
* Ending with a repeat of verse "A"

This song's format could thus be described as ABACADA. There are many variations, but at the core is the verse and refrain theme. Also, the verses and refrains may not be exact repeats of their predecessors, but are recognizable as similar segments.

The rondo is like a conversation between several different people. Musical instruments are the voices which are making statements and carrying on "conversations." This music format is good for all kinds of belly dance routines, from classic to modern, and for storytelling dances.

Theme and variations

Theme and variations describes a musical theme (phrase or bar of music upon which the rest of the song is based). The theme is repeated over and over, but with continuous variations, until the latter part of the music sounds totally different from the original phrase.

The classic European example of this format is Beethoven's Fifth Symphony. Beethoven took four simple notes, then changed them throughout his musical masterpiece, embellishing them to create many variations. The symphony which develops is full of emotion, drama and dynamics, but retains similar accents as the original four notes played in the first bar of music. Just as simple gestures can have the power to move us deeply into emotion, simple accents and rhythms have the power to move us deeply.

A theme and variations are sometimes found in short instrumental segments of belly dance songs, including many drum solos. This format is particularly effective during drumming, because Near Eastern rhythms are so beautifully embellished with many hand drumming techniques, such as drumrolls and accents.

Many drum solos begin with a simple rhythmic pattern, later evolving into complex, multi layered rhythms. The simple rhythmic pattern at the beginning feels like a simple gesture, and then the musicians take the listener on a journey into an Oriental design. The drumming becomes embellished and complex, like an Oriental carpet designed with intricate patterns and color variations.

Many songs have drum solo segments which use a theme and variations. A drum solo may begin with simple, unembellished versions of basic rhythms, building up into more complex and embellished versions of the rhythm, resulting in rhythmic highlights and climactic points.

Example:

- Simple rhythm played on a single drum *(theme)*.
- Simple rhythm with a few added accents *(variation 1)*.
- Embellished rhythm, a second instrument joins in *(variation 2)*.
- Rhythm speeds up. *(variation 3)*.

Suite

A *suite* is a song of three or more sections, played with different tempos and qualities. Some belly dance songs or sets of songs are played in this format.

A *suite* traditionally refers to a song consisting of:

- Medium tempo introduction.
- Slow middle section.
- Fast finale.

The moderate tempo of the introduction expresses feelings of energy and fun. The slower middle section takes us into feelings of big, slow movements and serious, profound emotions. During this slow section, the dancer may do floor-work or taqsim movements to reflect these feelings. Finally, the fast tempo of the finale communicates feelings of energy and excitement, and an energizing finale and "good-bye."

Listening for cues

When listening for a song's format, remember that a song could be a pure version of one of the forms, or a combination of more than one of form. Rondos are extremely common, with verse and chorus also being common in belly dance music.

Understanding the way music is formatted helps a dancer be prepared for upcoming changes in belly dance songs. Listening for changes in the tempo, lyrics or instrumentation is helpful when listening for format cues.

OPPOSITE: *Oracle demonstrates a tribal fusion style of dancing with a sword to a taqsim.*

Exercises:

Taqsim: Improvise a dance to a slow instrumental, standing in place (no traveling steps). Notice the patterns of your breathing as you perform slow movements. Next, dance to the same taqsim, but this time use traveling steps. Notice how the two experiences feel different. Did you enjoy one more than the other? Which was easier?

Analytical listening: Listen to any song with pen and paper in hand, then identify segments. Recognize where the introduction starts and ends, then listen for segments (taqsim, verses, choruses, drum solos, etc.).

- Identify the introduction.
- Next, write down letter "A" for the first segment you hear after the intro.
- At the next significant change in the music, assign the letter "B," and so on.
- If you hear a segment which is a repetition or near-repetition of a previous segment, assign it the same letter as you did its twin.
- At the end of the song, look at your written notation. What format is the song? Does the song fit into a particular format, or is it a combination of more than one format? Did you note segments based on instrumentation, tempo, or vocalist? (Example: A=singer, B=percussion, C= fast, D=wind instruments.)

Verse and chorus: Using finger cymbals (zils, sagat) or another percussion instrument, experiment with playing in the verse and chorus format, changing patterns during the song. Example (using cymbals): R refers to tone made by striking the right hand pair, L refers to tone from left hand:

Verse: Start with a repeating pattern or rhythm (example: RLRL).
Chorus: Play a different pattern or rhythm (example: RLR pause).

Verse: Repeat first verse or rhythm, or make a slight variation of first verse.
Chorus: Repeat chorus or rhythm (example: RLR pause).

Verse and chorus dance: Repeat the previous exercise, selecting a dance movement or combination of movements to dance as a verse, and a different set of movements for the chorus. This can be a group exercise (divide into groups A and B). A soloist can alternate different movement combinations, or alternate isolations of different parts of the body.

Call and reply (group exercise): With a friend, or several friends, take turns playing short rhythmic patterns with cymbals or other percussion instruments. Dancer #1 plays a short segment (example: RLR pause). Dancer #2 replies by mirroring the segment, or by responding with a different segment (example: RLRLRLR). Repeat calling and responding. This exercise helps develop variety in your cymbal playing by helping you discover new patterns and pleasing combinations of sounds.

Call and reply dance: As a class or group exercise (duets), divide into Groups 1 and 2. Group 1 selects movements and dances the verse, and Group 2 selects movements and dances the chorus. A soloist may also perform this format by using a step as the "call" and a different movement as the "reply."

Rondo instrumental: Playing the instrument of your choice, or using hand claps:

A: Start with a pattern or rhythm.
B: Play a new pattern or rhythm.
A: Repeat A.
C: Play a new pattern or rhythm
A: Repeat A.
D: Play a new pattern or rhythm.
A: Repeat A.

Rondo dance: Select movements or movement combinations and call them A, B, C, D. (Example: A=hip slide, B=head slide, C=shoulder accent, D=turn). Then dance: ABACADA.

Ternary instrumental: Repeat the rondo instrumental exercise, playing ABA instead of a rondo. Use new variations of patterns or rhythms. Next, using dance movements, dance ABA.

Theme and variations instrumental: Select a basic rhythm, then clap it with your hands or play it with your instrument. Next, create variations by changing it from loud to soft, fast to slow, and adding pauses.

Theme and variations: Select a geometric shape or dance movement combination, then continuously adapt it. (Example: start with a hip square, or step-hop combination.) Ideas for adaptation include making the shape or dance steps more simple, more complex, changing speed, height, level and direction of movements, or transferring a geometric design from one part of the body to another. In this exercise, you are abstracting from a theme.

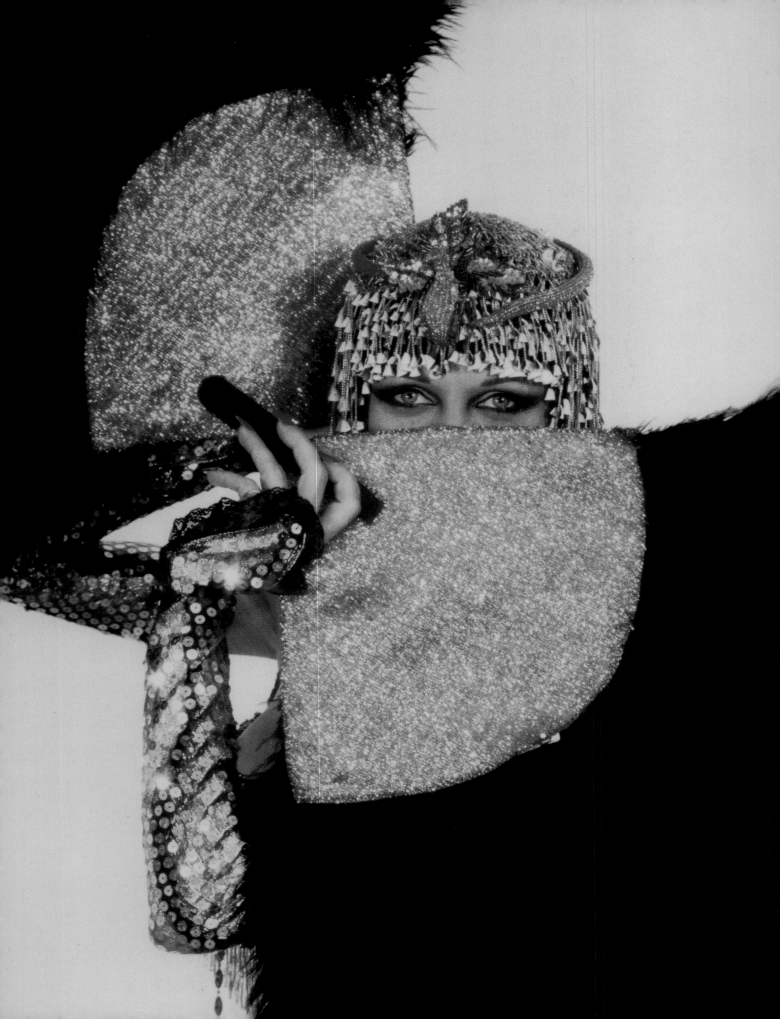

PART V

STUDENTS, TEACHERS AND AUDIENCES

OPPOSITE: *Dance students see their dreams onstage during performances by talented instructors. Audiences see magical moments of enchantment. Performers see affection and admiration in the eyes of the audience. (Photo of Coco courtesy of the artist.)*

CHAPTER FOURTEEN

Proven Techniques to Enhance your Learning Skills

"We are all masters, AND we are all students."

BILLY WOODS, DRUMMER, TEACHING A CLASS IN PENNSYLVANIA

*E*very successful professional in *any* business is continually involved with getting more training. Therefore, learning new techniques and gaining new information is crucial to growth as a dancer. Understanding how you learn helps you
absorb choreography faster, and how to teach others effectively.

Styles of learning and teaching aids

People learn new information in three ways: by *seeing, hearing* and *doing (feeling)*.
Most people have a preference among these three media. Think back on something new you did recently, dance-related or otherwise. Maybe you learned a
new dance movement or went to a new restaurant. Did you read about it in a
newspaper, book or a magazine (visual)? See it in a video or TV (visual)? Hear
about it from a friend (hearing)? Try a new movement that felt good, or felt an
urge for something new (feeling)? The way you typically answer these questions
may show your personal preference for how you learn: either by *seeing, hearing*
or *feeling*.

   Learning a dance step is easiest when all three are used together:

- *Verbally* breaking down and explaining the movement is auditory.
- *Demonstrating* the step gives the visual information.
- *Feeling* the movement in your own body by practicing the step is kinesthetic.

Touch technique

In addition, some teachers use the sense of touch to help their students understand movements. Valerie Larkin, a belly dance teacher in Dublin, Ireland, is

OPPOSITE: *It's fun to learn different approaches to belly dance and to wear different costume*
styles. The coin costume with the full skirt is worn with bare feet or flat sandals for performances
with an earthy feeling. (Photo of Ramona.)

blind, and uses the sense of touch to check her students' posture and movements.[37]

Other teachers use touch as a teaching aid by having students feel movements on the instructor's spine, shoulder, or hip. One of my teachers helped me understand a hip movement by putting her finger on the exact spot on my hip that needed to rotate. Suddenly the movement "clicked" for me.

The science of touch training: Touch training works because when your teacher touches the skin over your muscle, precise information is relayed to the sensory cortex of your brain to help you establish an image of which muscles to contract. In other words, you are developing an *engram* or "muscle memory." The "touch technique" is not restricted to dance movement; it is also effectively used by personal trainers in weightlifting exercises, and has broad application to other physical disciplines which require coordinated muscle movements.

Valerie uses the sense of touch to "see" her students' movements and to give them feedback. A touch on the spine tells her whether the student's alignment is correct. Sighted instructors use the touch technique also. A hearing-impaired student was unable to understand a particular hip movement until I placed her hand on my own hip during the muscle contraction. Suddenly her eyes lit up and she understood.

A word of caution: if you choose to use touch in your teaching, be sensitive to your student's preferences; some dancers do not like others to touch them. Respect their boundaries. Ask permission before touching, or explain/show without touching. Verbally explaining along with a visual demonstration of a movement is more effective with some students. In today's litigation-oriented society, there is still some discussion of how to resolve liability issues regarding touch training in the bodybuilding and weight-training community.

Another effective use of touch training is to tell students to place their *own* hand on the skin over where the muscle should be moving, to feel the contraction. This is great for large groups, where the teacher can't give individual feedback to everyone. I ask beginner students, *"Put your hand on the back of your hip—do you feel the muscle tighten?,"* during particular hip movements and warm-up exercises. I put my hand on my own hip to show them where they should be feeling the contraction. This ensures that they understand what they are doing with their muscles, and that they are not just visually mimicking the instructor's movements.

Touch training tip: Place a wooden box over a speaker or boom box. By placing a hand or foot on the box while the music plays, you can physically feel the underlying pulse of the music. Some multi layered belly dance songs have so many different instruments playing that it is difficult for some students to identify the basic underlying pulse. The wooden box transmits the pulse very well via varying levels of vibrations, which are felt with hands or feet. This technique is used in modern dance to help students who are tone-deaf or hearing-impaired, but it's very helpful for all other students too.

Proven ways of enhancing the learning experience

Encourage your students to take written notes, since putting ideas in their own words will reinforce their memory, and give an added visual and feeling cue.

Some teachers use visual cues as a teaching aid. A written list of movements and techniques is a helpful reminder of new material learned. I still refer to dance notes from a retreat I attended years ago. A particular favorite is one with simple stick figures of various poses; it is helpful for finding a pose to begin or end a dance with.

Instructional DVDs are helpful at-home sup-

DVDs are helpful learning tools, and illustrate artistic diversity among professional dancers.

plements to in-person classes with a teacher. Practicing at home is crucial for excellence in dance, and DVDs are helpful for learning new things and for practicing familiar movements. Performance DVDs are useful for giving dancers the opportunity to see many different styles and interpretations in various performance settings.

Years ago, I took purchased performance recordings to my local teacher, to ask for her help in understanding movements I'd seen on the tapes. The dancers on the tapes live a long way from us. Although my local teacher didn't dance the style of those far away performers, she was very helpful with breaking down the movements for me. (A tip she gave me for figuring out movements on recordings was to closely watch the changes in the dancer's weight placement on her feet.)

Books and magazines

Lastly, do not underestimate the usefulness of dance magazines and books as resources for dance training. Dance magazines help dancers stay current on news and trends, and are fun reading, containing useful tips and information.

The foremost dancers I know frequently talk about books which particularly inspired them. Ask a teacher you admire about the books she recommends. Reading a great book can change your dancing and your life forever. Books are portable, packed with information, and conveniently read bit-by-bit as time allows. I also encourage you to check out the dance and music books at your local public library.

Belly dance notebook, encyclopedia and gold file

A 3-ring binder is wonderful for keeping all your dance ideas, special magazine articles, news clippings, and miscellaneous dance-related papers neatly stored and organized. I use subject tabs such as "choreography," "movements," "dance history," "costumes" and "workshop notes" to file my papers. This helps when you need to find specific information in a hurry. You have your own Belly Dance Encyclopedia at your fingertips.

Also, a small, easy-to-tote notebook or voice recorder is a must-have for jotting down ideas and new information for future reference. You can transfer the contents of your notebook to your binder for long-term use.

Keep a *"Gold File"* of all your positive feedback. I labeled a file folder, where I keep special letters and treasured photos. Refer to it when you need a pick-me-up.

Shimmying free: style and individuality

While there is a real benefit to staying with a gifted teacher and learning a specific style for several years, it is fun to learn more than one style. However, it takes time, patience, and energy to master any style of dance. Instructors need to be well-versed in various aspects of belly dance technique and style, since students are mirroring them.

It has become popular to label a belly dancer. Examples of categories are: *Oriental, Tribal, Egyptian, Turkish, Fusion,* and many more. Labels are handy, but they can also be limiting.

I don't believe that people fall into neat little categories. Dance styles are like languages; one style is our "native" language, but we can be multi lingual too. Some students want a particular style of belly dance led by a specific instructor; other students are open to studying a variety of styles with a variety of teachers; and other students want to learn one particular style, but are open to studying with different teachers of that style.

A student aspiring to professional status needs to realize that, in deciding to focus on one dance style to the exclusion of all others, you are defining your talent in one term. For example, if you say that you are an "Egyptian style dancer" or a "Fusion dancer," you are implying that particular style is the *only* style you can do.

I believe that each of us is capable of many things and can express ourselves through more than one dance style, if we choose. On the other hand, a dancer may not be interested in studying more than one style, and that's a personal choice and a preference which suits many dancers.

Pros need to take into consideration whether staying within one style will affect their number of paid engagements, and thus their income. One of my friends complained that her selected dance style is not as popular as other styles, and she is convinced that this is the reason she is not offered as many teaching and performing jobs as she would like.

A male dancer who specializes in one dance form decided to start working out with weights to add muscle, then changed his costume style to show off his new look. These changes resulted in his being more employable, without changing anything about his dance technique. Another strategy for adding variety is to change costume styles and music selections to create a fresh new look.

I am reluctant to put a label on my style of dance (other than calling it "belly dance"), but since students have started asking me about my

OPPOSITE: *Style and individuality are shown by costuming, dance movements, poses, and more. (Photo of Ramona.)*

"style," I felt the need to call it something. I decided to call it "BellyDance American Style," because the dance movements I perform and teach come from a diverse background of training from instructors of many different styles of belly dance, and my jazz background too.

Style is very individual. Although I've studied with literally dozens of different belly dance teachers during the past 20+ years, there was one local teacher of Egyptian style dance with whom I studied for 10 years. When others saw me dance and liked my performance, they asked who my local teacher was, assuming that her way of dancing was like mine, and then went to her for lessons.

A friend and fellow instructor who studied with a different teacher overseas told me she had the same experience. These referrals were nice for our teachers, but neither of us is a "clone" of any particular instructor, and our resulting dance styles are very different from the way our mentors dance.

In the genre of modern dance, some students of accomplished dancers/choreographers are considered "apprentices," who studied technique and choreography with a master choreographer, then later formed their own dance companies, creating their own unique dance stylizations. This happens a lot in belly dance too. I feel that my friend and I were apprentices of our teachers, but our styles are uniquely our own. I look at the students I've mentored and see that their dance styles are quite different from mine. Although they use movements I taught, their overall approaches to dancing are uniquely their own, showing their own personality and flair.

Ultimately, a teacher who enables her students to create success for themselves promotes the art of belly dance in a far-reaching way, and encourages diversity within the art. It's up to you to decide what styles suit your interests best and make you happiest. If you dance professionally, then you need a plan for how to market your selected dance skills.

Exercises:

Learning: What is your preferred method of learning: seeing, hearing or doing? During your next dance class or group rehearsal, notice the preferences of other dancers. When teaching a class, be sure to use all three methods together when teaching something new.

Applied learning: Select any step or combination of steps which has been challenging for you. Repeat the step slowly:

- Talk yourself through the step out loud (count "1, 2, 3 . . ." or say right/left when stepping). *(Auditory approach.)*
- Watch yourself in the mirror while doing the step. *(Visual approach.)*
- Dance the step several times, paying close attention to how the movement feels in each part of the body. Notice weight shifting in the feet, and feelings in the arms, shoulders, belly and back. *(Kinesthetic approach.)*
- Evaluate which of the above practice methods was most helpful to you.

Using a different approach: There are different approaches to seeing, hearing, and doing. Some dancers like for steps and facing directions to be called out loud (auditory and analytical). Others are not concerned with counting, but are interested in movement patterns and how steps feel (kinesthetic and spatial).

Sometimes your less-preferred method of learning is helpful with learning new approaches and mastering unfamiliar movements. Experiment with using your less-preferred method on challenging movements, and see whether it helps you during the learning process.

As an example, I've always preferred *not* counting steps. (I am inclined to pay more attention to how steps feel, a kinesthetic approach.) Through many years of belly dancing, ballet, jazz, and folk dance performances, I memorized choreography by remembering the sequence of steps and patterns, but never counted.

Teaching belly dance classes forced me to learn to count steps aloud, since many students want the counts of each step called aloud when learning new combinations. I've noticed that counting aloud also helps *me* learn unfamiliar movements and simplifies step combinations when I'm taking a workshop that someone else is teaching. Counting aloud does not come naturally to me, and is a skill I've had to work on. Do you have a skill that you want to develop?

Magazines: Look at fashion, hair, celebrity, or other magazines in your local public library. Current magazines show trends in makeup, hairstyling and clothing styles which may give you useful ideas to update your own look onstage. Makeup trends vary seasonally, along with clothing trends. If you don't already subscribe to a belly dance magazine, consider doing so (see Resources). Some free online magazines are also full of interesting articles and helpful dance tips.

CHAPTER FIFTEEN

The Business of Teaching Bellydancing

"It is the supreme art of the teacher to
awaken joy in creative expression and knowledge."

ALBERT EINSTEIN (1879–1955)

$\mathcal{B}$eing a dance instructor is a life-enriching experience. *"You get back so much more than you give,"* Kalila, an Atlanta instructor, told me. It is a joy to see your students understand a new movement. It is also a very special experience to help others get in touch with their bodies, and realize their potential in unexpected ways. Students discover muscles that they didn't know existed, and they learn that they have untapped creative talent. Dancing gives us more appreciation of our physical and creative capabilities, and enhances our self-image and confidence.

Dancing as a full-time or part-time career

Some belly dancers earn their living by teaching and performing. They are, however, more the exception than the rule. Performing and teaching dance is generally not well paid, and is listed among the lower paying professions in U.S. salary surveys.[38]

Most American belly dancers have a job besides dance that pays the bills. There is a handy term for this now: *dual-careerist*. Conversely, a gifted dancer can excel, and many talented dancers make a living solely through dance-related activities. Having an experienced performer or teacher mentor you in deciding how you want to pursue a career is extremely valuable in this situation.

Dancing for a living is challenging, and the individuals who do this benefit the dance community at large with their efforts to promote dance and their high standards of performance. If you decide to go full-time as a dancer, carefully consider the area in which you intend to live. Some regions are more supportive of the arts than others. A full-time pro told me she chose to open her dance school in California for this reason.

In addition to dancing at parties, restaurants and other paying venues, some dancers and instructors pursue their love of dance by making instructional and

OPPOSITE: *Presentation and public speaking skills are important in many situations. Ramona during a TV interview at her studio. The story featured an interview and a mini lesson, and aired on an Atlanta station. The reporter (at left) borrowed a costume for the show.*

performance recordings to sell. Some dancers enjoy using their business skills to sponsor workshops. Others are passionate amateurs who develop their dance skills without the pressure of making it into a paying profession, and find this approach gratifying. There are many choices and options for pursuing your love of dance.

Belly dance satisfies a need for creative self-expression, glamour and recognition that some of us don't get in our other jobs. It's interesting to see a talented dancer on a stage and later hear *"she's a chemist"* or *"she's an accountant."*

An advantage to dancing part-time is that dance stays fresh and exciting. Any full-time job has its periods where it becomes tiring, and dancing is a physically and emotionally demanding career. A therapist with a full-time schedule remarked that when he changed to working part-time, the quality of his service to his clients went up. He had more energy and felt less drained with a part-time workload. This can be true of dancing also.

On the other hand, full-time dancers have more time available to practice and perform, and therefore can develop their skills faster than most part-time dancers. One of my friends in Europe who dances for a living said that every morning she puts on music and practices steps for two hours. I saw her dance in a show where she was the only full-time pro, and saw a striking difference in skill level between her and the dancers who were part-time. Her two hours of daily practice were apparent.

Developing teaching skills

One of the most gifted dance teachers I know says that "teaching is a *big* responsibility." A teacher of *any* subject can be a great inspiration or a huge discouragement to a student. Most of us remember experiences with schoolteachers who either enhanced us or discouraged us. These impressions contribute to a student's success or failure. Instilling self-confidence and good tech-

nique in your dance students is important, because success repeats itself.

If you are interested in teaching dance classes, you need to work on developing and enhancing communication skills. Observe how classes are run by different teachers. Reading books on the subject is helpful too. *The Art of Teaching Dance Technique* and *The Super Studio: The Guide to a Successful Dance Studio!* are useful books (see Resources section).

Successful professional dancers also continue to be students. This is true of all dance forms. Continuing to enhance your own skills as a student is vital. As a student, you not only learn the movements your teachers are explaining, but you also observe *how* the movements are being taught, which helps you when instructing your own students.

The legendary dancer Nadia Gamal said, *"I have been a professional dancer for over 35 years and still feel like a student. An artist can never stop learning, because art has no borders."*

Presentation skills

One of the most important, but often neglected, how-to's of teaching is presentation skills: your gestures, your stance, your voice, your speaking habits when teaching. I recommend using a video camera to tape yourself teaching a class. In the absence of a video camera, ask a friend to take random pictures of you while teaching a class. Afterwards, look at the resulting pictures and ask yourself the following:

- What are your speech and gesture habits?
- Do you smile?
- Does your voice have variation, including loud, soft, fast, slow words?
- Are you making eye contact with your students?
- Are there verbal distractions, like overuse of "uh," "okay," "uh-huh?"

A belly dance class with Ramona. Having a "costume night" or dress rehearsal helps students find out how the costume works with their dance and whether alterations are needed. Plus, it's fun to dance in costume!

- Are you standing rooted like a tree, or are you moving around, making contact with your whole group?
- Do you occasionally pause when you're speaking, in order to emphasize a point?
- Do you use effective gestures to illustrate the meaning of your words?

The video camera is an objective observer that shows you what you're doing. When you become aware of undesirable speech habits, then you can change them.

If you have access to individual or group training for public speaking, this can help you with *all* your business-related speaking skills, including teaching dance classes. A situation where you get one-on-one feedback from a communications trainer is ideal.[39]

As a teacher, you are also a performer and a presenter of information. You have the job of verbal explanation, visual demonstration, and giving verbal feedback to your students. When teaching, I feel that I am on an informal stage. I am showing, telling and giving feedback to a group of students all at once. They are my audience, who have come to see me demonstrate, lead them in dance move-

ment, speak to them about their progress and help them to develop a new skill.

Good presentation skills by the teacher are absolutely vital to effective instruction. Novelist Gail Godwin said, *"Good teaching is one-fourth preparation and three-fourths theater."* Very true!

Business skills

Belly dance teachers are in a service industry. We offer a "service" (classes), and in return we get paid by "customers" (students). *Always remember that your students and your sponsors are your customers, and treat them that way!*

Most students are attending classes to learn something new and to have fun, and these two needs must be satisfied. If you're advertising a workshop based on requests to teach a special veil technique, you need to make sure your students walk away afterwards with the knowledge that they came for.

Some students have complained about attending belly dance workshops and coming back with jazz or yoga training, when what they were seeking was new belly dance technique. It literally pays to fulfill people's expectations. Make sure you give people what they're expecting; be sure that your advertising is a clear representation of what you are offering.

How do you know how you're doing as a teacher?

Some belly dance teachers charge $60 or more per hour for professional feedback and coaching on dance technique. *Feedback on your teaching technique is just as valuable and is free for the asking!*

Besides observing your student's progress in class, you may want to ask for anonymous opinions. On occasion, I hand out a one page critique sheet that asks for ratings (from 1-5) about "effectiveness of teaching," "music," "helpfulness of handouts," and so on. Students circle the number that applies. They fill out this questionnaire on the last night of the class session. It only takes a few minutes to complete the survey, and they turn in their sheets when they leave the classroom.

The survey also has a few open-ended questions, which are the most helpful part of the survey for me, because the answers give me specifics:

- What did you like most about this class?
- What did you like least?
- What specific topics you are interested in learning (cymbals, veils, etc.)?
- How could this class be improved?
- Blank space for general comments.

Students are generally too polite to give negative criticism verbally, and the anonymous feedback sheet gives you the opportunity to get candid responses and helpful suggestions. Remember that you can't please all of the people all of the time. One negative comment may not indicate that the whole class was dissatisfied. Instead, look for general trends in the comments. For example, since I had several people write that they'd like to learn how to play finger cymbals, the next class session focused on cymbal technique.

Getting feedback helps you know what you're doing right, and it's important to feel appreciated after you've put all the hard work into teaching and preparing for a class. Positive quotes from students are also useful for advertising brochures.

Negative feedback

Negative feedback tells us how we can improve. Being on the receiving end of criticism is never easy, but it can be just as valuable as positive feedback. If you earn your income mainly through dance-related activities, it's important to know whether your customers are happy, and find ways to make them happy if they are not. Marketing research has shown that one dissatisfied customer will tell *ten* other people about their bad experience with a company or service provider!

On the other hand, if you don't want to make any changes to your classes after receiving negative feedback, you are *not* obligated to do so. At a minimum, you will find out how to better advertise your classes and events to reach your target audience or customers. You may need to direct advertising to a different group of potential customers. For example, one teacher I know changed her class description from "Belly dance" to "Belly dance movement meditation," since the latter more accurately describes what she teaches.

Advertising

Part of a service provider's job is to fulfill the customer's expectations. This is true for every profession, from medical doctors to performing artists. Let prospective customers know what to expect from you.

Also consider expanding your advertising to encompass those non-dancers who are interested in your specific topic, for example "dance meditation." For example, advertisements in yoga journals or New Age websites could potentially reach students who are interested in meditation, and who may be interested in learning dance meditation. This could be a new way to draw more students into your classes.

The bottom line is that dance teachers and performers are in the business of selling good feelings through dance. The level of skill, talent and communication they have contribute to their success. In addition, a successful business person must be ethical, professional, and genuinely considerate of other people's feelings. *This may ultimately be more important to success than how skilled a dancer and instructor they are!*

The personality factor is important in *all* professions which involve human interaction, and dance is no exception. There is no business that is *not* show business, and an important part of a show or class is the pre-event advertising and communication with prospective customers!

Communicating with students

I encourage students to take classes and workshops from a variety of belly dance teachers, particularly at the intermediate and advanced levels, so that they may learn different approaches and styles. I follow up by asking students to let me know how their classes work out with the other teachers. What I hear most is that students at every level need nurturing and encouragement, and this is particularly crucial at the intermediate and advanced levels. Students want a teacher who has a positive attitude and is patient and helpful.

Remember that belly dance teachers are in the business of selling good feelings through dance. Our students are not required by the public school system to take belly dance classes; most attend for fun, fellowship, recreation and sometimes for physical fitness.

Even at the advanced and professional levels, students expect more than just learning new techniques and choreography. They also expect a degree of genuine concern and caring on the part of the instructor. We're all human with the accompanying emotional needs.

However, many students want to try out belly dance classes for a short time, and are not interested in becoming intermediate/advanced level dancers. Beginner-level classes are very important for many reasons.

Beginner-level students may refer their friends for classes after they've had a positive experience. Sometimes they are students of other dance forms or people trying to get fit, or they're looking for something new to try for a few weeks. In this case, you are the only dance teacher they ever have. The knowledge you give them about dance over the course of a few weeks may last a lifetime.

Appreciation

How do you make students feel appreciated? First, *learn everyone's name.* At the start of a session of beginner classes, I ask each student to introduce themselves and say what interested them about the class. This ice-breaking technique helps me get an idea of what they're expecting or looking to learn, so that I can better meet their needs. Also, they find out something interesting about all their classmates. Every class has a unique mix of interesting people.

Praise students individually and as a group for things they are doing correctly. In general, people don't give or receive enough praise or encouragement. There is always something praiseworthy about each student.

Never be humorous at someone else's expense. It's surprising how a remark can be misconstrued. We can forgive people for almost any transgression except rudeness, bad grammar and body odor! People may forget what you said or did, but they will never, ever forget how you made them feel.

This brings us to another common sense finding of marketing research: *it's easier and takes less advertising dollars to get repeat customers than to solicit new business.* In practical terms, this means serving your current customers well.

Helping your students

Compliment them as appropriate on their achievements, their costumes, their exercise attire, and anything else they do well or deserve credit for. Be interested in them and provide quality service: clear instruction, good technique, precise feedback and corrections, catch them doing something right and tell them so. Above all, make them feel appreciated.

Select your teaching philosophy. While in California several years ago, I spent a week taking advanced classes from a teacher there, and was surprised at how different they were from the advanced classes I'd been taking locally. One had a grueling warm-up, the other a low-key stretching warm up; one was basically a drill, where various movements were rehearsed repeatedly, while the other a class focused on inventing and perfecting new movements; one class was done all on the balls of the feet, the other class mainly flat-footed in the folkloric style. Both classes had merit.

I decided on a "fun and informative" approach to teaching my classes, with a focus on learning dance movements, a choreographed dance, and developing improvisational and choreography skills to enable students to create their own dances. My beginner-level classes at local parks and recreation facilities have a wide range of students, many of whom are curious and want to learn a little about belly dance, but are not "serious" ongoing students. I provide fun dances, a little dance history and cultural background information, explanation of movement theory, and sometimes a recital at a local restaurant or a "field trip" (class attendance at a local belly dance show or similar event). The class is challenging, but it's not a test of endurance.

Finally, remember that the best thing you can do for your students is to keep learning new things yourself. As teachers, we are also perpetual students of the art. Serious belly dancers need to study at least one other form of movement. Ballet, jazz, yoga, hip-hop, Latin dance and flamenco have all influenced belly dance in this modern age, and will continue to do so in the future.

Belly dance is also influencing other dance forms. For example, one of my students is a certified country line dancing instructor who creates dances for club performances and country western dance competitions. She fuses country line dancing with belly dance by adding snake arms and undulations to her traveling steps in line dances, performing in rhinestone-studded jeans and cowboy boots! Another of my students is a professional choreographer and Christian worship dance instructor, fusing belly dance with worship dance and performing in white liturgical dance costumes at churches.

The music, costuming and steps of country line dances and Christian worship dances are totally different from traditional belly dance, yet belly dance adds a feminine and meaningful flair to these performances. Belly dance fusion with other styles is becoming more common in our multi cultural society, and teachers need to be aware of the trends.

Every student has unique talent

A valuable piece of advice given me by a master teacher is to *"treat students like they're intelligent, and they will be."* Students can understand almost all movements with a verbal and visual breakdown of the technique, clear demonstration, feedback from the teacher, and enough repetition and home practice.

Sometimes verbally describing a movement in a different way is enough to help a student understand. One teacher helped me learn a challenging hip movement by describing it differently. Her approach was new to me and instantly helped me to understand.

Recognize your students as the intelligent people they are. Part of respecting your students means believing in their ability to learn. If they are having problems learning something, take another look at how you're teaching it, and approach it from a different perspective.

Belly dancing for fun and profit

I've met many workshop instructors who are nice, competent dancers, with expert technique and a businesslike attitude. These people are extremely successful and have large followings. This is because their teaching has exceptional clarity, they're willing to share information freely, they are friendly and pleasant, they realize that students are their customers, they act appropriately, and they appreciate their sponsors. Their personality and their professionalism largely contribute to their success.

Sponsors are customers too, and like all other customers, they want smooth, easy and profitable business dealings, and they want to feel appreciated. Event sponsorship is a very tough job and a time-consuming labor. Supporting the sponsors in your dance community is important, to keep future events coming.

A successful teacher on the international workshop circuit said that part of her mission is to ensure the *sponsor's* success at her workshops. She wants to help the sponsor make a profit and have a successful event, so that everyone will have good memories and that she will be asked to return. This is a reminder that it's easier to get a repeat customer than it is to solicit new business. There is much more to teaching dance than just dancing. Personality and professionalism are crucial.

For your contemplation:

Presentation skills: Watch or listen to a recording of yourself. It is important to be aware of speaking habits you use in everyday life, for success in business and personal communication. If you are a teacher it's very helpful to watch a recording of a class you've taught. Observe your voice variety (loud, soft, fast, slow), pauses in speech, gestures and eye contact, and then answer the following questions:

- What overall impression do you give?
- Are your cues and instructions clear?
- What do you like about your communication style?
- What would you like to change?
- Do you have a favorite public speaker or performer from whom you can get ideas?

Voice variety: Follow my voice coach's suggestion for enhancing voice variety: read easy books aloud (including children's books) making sure to include loud, soft, fast and slow words, and pauses for emphasis. This exercise helps us become more accustomed to using voice variety during daily conversations, to avoid speaking in a monotone.

Advertising: How do you currently advertise your business? Have you set your budget for advertising? What options do you have within your budget for additional advertising (magazine ads, flyers, etc.)? Are you happy with your current level of business engagements and feel no need for additional advertising?

Cross-training: Professional dancers and teachers need to study other forms of physical movement to enhance their skills. Cross-training helps performing artists avoid burnout, and to learn new techniques and approaches. Select another genre to study: ballet, jazz, yoga, Pilates, Latin dance, flamenco or any other form that interests you. Sign up for a class or check your local library for instructional books or DVDs you can work with at home.

Positive attitude: Find something positive to say to each person you meet today. There is something praiseworthy about each student and business acquaintance that you meet.

CHAPTER SIXTEEN

Communication Between Dancer and Audience

"I dance for myself, not the audience."

NADIA GAMAL (1937–1990), INTERNATIONAL ORIENTAL DANCE STAR

One of the most satisfying aspects of the art of belly dance is the unlimited potential for personal growth and creativity. Every person sees every work of art differently. Two people looking at the same Renoir painting will have varying opinions of it, and two people watching the same dance performance will have varying opinions of it.

You can't please all the people all the time

While audiences may share the same general opinion of a dance concert, they are guaranteed to have vastly divergent differences of opinions of it regarding other aspects. For example, everyone in the audience may recognize that it was an expensively-costumed, well-rehearsed, well-lighted work, but have completely different opinions about whether they liked it or not.

Some may remember it as the best concert they ever attended; others think it was well done but left them unmoved emotionally; others believe it was low-quality compared to other concerts they've seen. There are likely to be as many different opinions as there are members of the audience.

Performances of any kind, whether they are in a movie theater or on a concert stage, are seen by each person differently, because we each see the performance *through the lens of our individual experiences and expectations.* That's how art is supposed to be!

Example:

I had a conversation with an acquaintance about a major West Coast dance concert. She and I sat across an aisle from each other, seeing the same concert at the same angle at the same time. Later I told a close friend, a gifted dance teacher, about this conversation, and she saw a third aspect of the performance that neither I nor my acquaintance recognized:

OPPOSITE: *Saroya performing in an Atlanta restaurant.*

STUDENTS, TEACHERS AND AUDIENCES

What I saw:

- One of the dancers particularly impressed me. She was a mature woman who had strong communication with the audience using gestures and facial expressions. I saw her dance as a moving and strong expression of mature womanly strength expressed by the upper body. I also saw her confidence, her years of experience as a dancer, and the career history she'd created reflected in her movements.

What my acquaintance saw:

- My acquaintance sarcastically remarked that the dancer "didn't dance." She, and many other dancers in the audience, was disappointed by the performance.

What my teacher friend recognized:

- She commented that I was watching the body of the *entire* dancer, while my acquaintance was watching only the dancer's *hips*. My friend remarked that many dancers, when sitting in the audience, are concerned mainly with what the hips are doing, nearly to the exclusion of everything else. In other words, if the hips aren't moving, they believe the dancer is not dancing. (The dancer in question has knee injuries which limit her hip articulations.)

Conclusion:

- My acquaintance and I saw the same performance simultaneously, and yet we literally saw *different* performances! Neither of us was "right" or "wrong" in our opinions. Each of us was personal and subjective in our opinions.

I've had similar conversations with other friends.[40] We need to recognize that individual viewers have vastly different opinions, and there-fore we need to take critiques we receive with consideration, but also with a grain of salt. Some criticism may be constructive and useful to us, while other comments may not be. We are also usually much more critical of ourselves than any other critic would ever be.

Every individual has unique preferences, and trying to please every audience member would be futile. To excel at what they do, an artist follows her or his own individual preferences, and does their best. By doing this, personal satisfaction, respect from audiences and peers and (hopefully) commercial success follows.

Be nice to yourself and others, especially when evaluating performances. Recognize that every dancer is special, and that there is no "right" or "wrong" when it comes to how an individual feels about a dance. Any decisions about changing or not changing a choreography or improvisation are up to the dancer, troupe or choreographer, and not the viewers! Listen to feedback, pay attention to your instincts, and make your own decisions.

Viewing recorded performances

Remember that DVD and videotaped recordings are 2-dimensional representations of a 3-dimensional experience, and therefore are not precisely accurate reflections of what happened in the moment. Kalila reminded me that a recording lacks the emotional connection of a live performance.

Video quality makes a huge difference in the way a performance looks. One of my friends was upset about a recording of her performance; she performed a dance of small, articulated hip movements, and the camera recorded her from across the room. From this perspective, she said it looked as though she was "doing nothing." The videographer was also sloppy in his recording, not taking close-ups and not keeping her in the viewfinder. However, a second camera in the front row did catch the nuances of her dance. She felt much better when seeing the second recording. This is a good example of seeing the same performance, yet paradoxically seeing different performances.

Recordings are powerful tools for identifying movement habits and seeing performances from a distanced perspective. View recordings of yourself as a tool for growth, and not as a critic! Look for the things that you did that you liked, besides the things that you'd like to change. Making recordings of practice sessions may also be helpful. Review these to evaluate progress toward your goals.

Having a skilled teacher view your recordings and give you objective feedback is extremely helpful. At Oasis Dance Camp, I met with Cassandra for a critique of one of my performance recordings. Her objective comments and observations picked up on elements that I did not see, and she made several helpful suggestions for areas I needed to work on. Also, when I mentioned things I saw about my own performance that I didn't like but wasn't sure how to fix, she gave me helpful suggestions for those areas as well. I've also had video critiques with other instructors, and in every case the feedback has been extremely helpful. Video critiques have been so useful for me that I encourage others to do this with instructors of their choice.

Regional aesthetics

Dancing for an American audience is different from dancing for a British audience, is different from dancing for an Egyptian audience, and is different from dancing for a Turkish audience. Artistic tastes differ regionally regarding preferred music, dance style, costume style and length of performance.

For example, in a restaurant in metro Atlanta, Georgia, customers are accustomed to seeing a belly dancer perform a set of dances for them for about 5-15 minutes, usually with recorded music, occasionally with a small band. After this, she takes a break, waits a while, and returns to dance another set once or twice more. In Cairo, Egypt, the dancer in a similar restaurant has a full band and dances for an hour before taking a break. Americans are accustomed to short performances, and are not as leisurely at the dinner table as Europeans and Egyptians.

Furthermore, dancing for an audience in a large concert setting is different from dancing for a corporate audience or an audience at a nursing home, elementary school, women's church group or at someone's house party. Each of these groups has different expectations.

What all groups have in common is that they want an entertaining performance that leaves them feeling good. Remember that the entertainment business is based on selling good feelings to customers.

Entertainment and artistry

When you are being paid to do a job, whether it's teaching a dance class, performing on a stage or working a desk job, it literally pays to fulfill the customer's and employer's expectations. In the art of belly dance, it is important that the performing artist gets personal gratification from her own performance as well. Both the customer and the artist can have their needs fulfilled at the same time; the customer's desire to be entertained and the artist's need to self-express *merge* during a performance.

A successful jazz musician commented that while he hopes the audience will like his music, their opinion is not his first consideration. His attitude is that he does his best effort, *for his own gratification*, and puts it out there for the world to see. Either audiences will like his music, or they won't. If they like it, that's great; if they don't like it, he can live with that too.

Many successful dancers share this opinion, though I've heard it expressed differently.

For example:

Carolena Nericcio, director of FatChanceBel-lyDance, remarked that initially her troupe's American Tribal Style (ATS) performances at belly dance festivals received mixed reactions. ATS was new and unique, and some audiences loved the style, and some audiences did not.[41] Over time ATS became extremely popular, and now is an integral part of the belly dance community and a well-loved form of entertainment for audiences worldwide. *But*, if this group had danced in a style to please all their audiences, rather than following their own preferences, their style would not have been unique, and this level of success would likely not have happened!

A male soloist remarked that when he was focusing on the audience, dancing was not so enjoyable for him. When he started being attentive to his own feelings while dancing, instead of focusing on the viewers, it was liberating. Another dancer remarked that when performing, he was too busy dancing to pay attention to the audience.[42] Both these dancers had successful careers by satisfying their own artistic needs first and letting go of the need for validation from an audience.

Self-Expression

Ultimately, the most important audience when you are dancing is *you*. Dance is a deep form of self expression, from the movements you choose to the way you put them together, to your gestures and facial expressions which express your personality. Your costume is also an important part of your unique expression.

Like language, dance is a form of personal communication. If you went to a meeting with a group of bankers, you'd dress in business attire, and if you went to an elementary school to talk to a kindergarten class, you'd dress differently. In each situation, you would use different words and

different clothes, but you'd still be expressing *your* ideas.

Be true to yourself. Here is a final thought on letting go of the need for other people's approval:

Mother Teresa's "Anyway"

"People are often unreasonable, irrational, and self-centered. Forgive them anyway. If you are kind, people may accuse you of selfish, ulterior motives. Be kind anyway. If you are successful, you will win some unfaithful friends and some genuine enemies. Succeed anyway. If you are honest and sincere people may deceive you. Be honest and sincere anyway. What you spend years creating, others could destroy overnight. Create anyway. If you find serenity and happiness, some may be jealous. Be happy anyway. The good you do today, will often be forgotten. Do good anyway. Give the best you have, and it will never be enough. Give your best anyway. In the final analysis, it is between you and God. It was never between you and them anyway."

In closing

I wish you a joyful journey of dynamic dance-making and performing!

Exercises:

Reviewing recordings of your own performances: Be kind to yourself. As performers, we are also sometimes our own worst critics. Both an intermediate student and an internationally-acclaimed dancer I interviewed confided that it is difficult for them to watch recordings of themselves. Others love to watch recordings of themselves. Some students, particularly beginners, said that they do not like to see themselves in the mirror when practicing.

OPPOSITE: *A soloist's costume should reflect her preferences and be appropriate for the setting of the dance. Photo of Aquilah courtesy of the artist.*

When we see ourselves, we may focus on what we could have done better, rather than seeing the positive aspects of what we did do. When viewing a recording of yourself, look for the things about your performance that you liked, as well as the aspects you want to change.

Compare notes for fun: Watch a recorded or live performance with a friend and discuss it afterward. What do you and your friend agree on? Did your friend see an aspect of the performance you didn't see? Did sharing your thoughts with someone else help give you insight into dance performances that you hadn't before considered?

Read reviews: Read reviews of belly dance DVDs, videos and music in dance magazines or online at dance websites. These reviews are usually informative about details of the production, regardless of whether or not you share the author's opinion of the performance. I've read bad reviews of what I considered outstanding performances, and great reviews of what I considered average performances.

The lesson learned is not to take other people's opinions too seriously. Reading bad reviews of outstanding performances by top dancers helped me learn to let go of the need for other people's approval in my own work. At times, reviews are genuinely helpful in giving information and an objective critique, while often you learn more about the author's preferences than you learn about the performance. In either case, it's interesting to see another person's perspective. However, your opinion of yourself is the most important opinion of all, because it flavors your every step.

Communication observation: Watch a dance performance (recorded or live), particularly observing gestures and eye contact. Is the dancer or troupe dancing to entertain *you*, or are they dancing for themselves in their own world while you observe? Which way do *you* want to dance? Do you want to do both?

Costume and music selections: Your costume needs to express your preferences and be appropriate for the setting of the dance. For example, a simple black cabaret costume would be appropriate on many concert stages and in restaurant performances. However, dancing at an elementary school festival would require a colorful costume with a daywear look (rather than the eveningwear look of many cabaret costumes). Also, dancing in a formal stage setting increases the audience's expectations of professional-level costuming. What kind of costume and music would you use for the following performance situations?

- Afternoon outdoor festival or large corporate picnic.
- Elementary school festival.
- In the privacy of your home.
- Wedding reception.
- Daytime event at a nursing home.
- Evening workshop or restaurant performance for a group of dancers.
- Formal concert performance.

Endnotes:

1. This popular group is much in demand for performances and has a busy schedule. They also use improvisation extensively.

2. Ibrahim (Bobby) Farrah (1939-1998), renowned master of Oriental dance and publisher of Arabesque Magazine, resided in New York City. He was internationally recognized for his excellent work in teaching, performing and choreographing. The IbrahimFarrah.com website has additional information.

3. *Blood Memory* by Martha Graham.

4. *Ibid.*

5. Suhaila.com website has an archive of newsletters which include insight about emotional aspects of dancing.

6. *Dance Teacher Magazine* April 2004, "Dance healthy, Dance smart" article.

7. *Blood Memory* by Martha Graham.

8. New Orleans workshop circa 1988.

9. *Ibid.*

10. My favorite instructional DVDs for floorwork are "Delilah's Belly Dance Workshop Vol. 3" (Visionarydance.com), "Classic Cabaret Floor Work with Anaheed" (Bellydance.org) and "Floor Moves and Advice" by Corey Zamora (Bellydancingonvideo.com).

11. A striking example of an effective "on the spot" dance was performed by a soloist who staged her dance with a spotlight focusing on her abdomen. The rest of the stage was in darkness. She performed a variety of hip movements which caused a chain reaction of movements in her abs. Members of the audience said the abdominal dance they saw was mesmerizing.

12. Shown in "Dances of Ecstacy" DVD.

13. Shown in "Delilah's Belly Dance Workshop Vol. 3" (Visionarydance.com) DVD.

14. *Emotions Revealed* by Paul Ekman.

15. Happiness, anger, disgust, sorrow, contempt, fear and surprise. Details of these facial expressions are shown in *Emotions Revealed* by Paul Ekman.

16. Tribal Basics Volume 4 (FCBD.com) and Delilah's Belly Dance Workshop Volume 3 (Visionarydance.com) are DVDs which explain the diaphragm flutter technique. *Pelvic Power* by Eric Franklin goes into detail about the relationship between the diaphragm and the pelvic floor. It explains the integrated relationships between various parts of the body and the pelvic floor using imagery, rather than approaching pelvic floor exercises as isolations. *Relax your neck and liberate your shoulders* by Franklin describes relationships between parts of the body (including the diaphragm) and the shoulders.

17. New Orleans workshop circa 1988.

18. This dance was distributed on videotape and therefore was seen by many dancers outside Egypt. *Habibi Magazine* Volume 18, No. 3 interview with Nagwa Fouad titled "An Uncommon Woman: Nagwa Fouad, Queen of Oriental Dance," includes a description of this dance and other works.

19. These initial ideas evolved into a dance which was so successful that the choreographer got a job teaching worship dance at a fine art academy as a result. The congregation thought her solo and her students group dances were "incredible," and the church leaders decided to include worship dance in the church's ongoing activities, with her as the director. She also began teaching worship dance workshops as a result of this performance. For more information about Christian worship dance, go to Psalm121.ca website.

20. Although swords manufactured for belly dancing are blunt-edged, some are quite heavy and come to a point. A few dancers have experienced bad injuries due to dropping a sword on their foot. Good technique and constant awareness are necessary to handle the sword safely. As with any prop, it's best to get a private lesson or take a group class to learn the basics of dancing with the sword. Corey Zamora's instructional "Sword and Tray Balancing for Bellydancers" DVD (Bellydancingonvideo.com) is helpful too.

21. GildedSerpent.com online magazine has articles with detailed information about glass dancing.

22. These are props for balancing on the head and on other parts of the body. A Russian dancer pours a little wine out of her glass at the end of her dance to show the audience that the wineglass truly contains liquid. I've also seen an Ohio dancer use a ketchup bottle for balancing, so ideas are limitless!

23. Several award-winning U.S. performing and teaching artists I spoke with said this how their choreography comes about. However, the intuitive approach is definitely *not* a one-size-fits-all approach. It works great for some dancers, and not at all for others.

24. *Habibi Magazine* Volume 18, No. 3 article "An Uncommon Woman: Nagwa Fouad, Queen of Oriental Dance."

25. Workshop taught by Mahmoud Reda as part of the Second International Conference on Middle Eastern Dance in 2001 at Orange Coast College in California.

26. Performed at Delilah's Visionary Bellydance Retreat in 1998.

27. *Dances of Ecstacy* DVD shows a *hadra*.

28. Nadia Gamal performed a Zar-based dance in Lebanon years ago. More recently, a few American and Canadian cabaret dancers began including Zar dances in some concert performances. Gildedserpent.com website has an interesting article titled *"The Zar"* by Yasmin which gives further details about the *hadra*.

29. *Birthing From Within* by Pam England and Rob Horowitz discusses the body/mind connection in detail.

30. A dancer told me that she was once performing with a live band, and that the singer used a song about a cute lamb on its way to someone's dinner plate. She didn't speak the language, and did not realize the lyrics were inappropriate until a distressed member of the audience came to her afterwards and told her that she needed to have a talk with the band about their song selections.

31. There is no singer with a status equal to Egypt's Uum Kalthoum in American or European culture. Uum Kalthoum was the most influential singer of the twentieth century in the Middle East. *The Voice of Egypt: Umm Kulthum, Arabic Song, and Egyptian Society in the Twentieth Century* by Virginia Danielson is a detailed biography and interesting reading. Many brief biographies and discographies are available online at various websites, and are easily found with a search engine.

32. The Chronicles Magazine Volume 4, Issue 2 "So What Else is New (Old)?" by Morocco, definition of *maksoum* has further details. Also, CD liner notes from Dance with Fifi Abdo CD *Shake Me Ya Gamal, Hot Tabla Solos* includes information regarding the history and use of rhythms, and is great for dancing.

33. Suhaila Dance Company DVDs (Suhaila.com) have recordings of troupe cymbal dances. Z-Helene's "Zils!" DVD (Zhelene.com) is a helpful how-to for intermediate and advanced cymbal players, and also shows an impressive zil solo.

34. Suhaila discussed this during a workshop taught in Charleston, SC in 2005.

35. Another traditional instrument is a set of four wooden spoons (*kashiklar*), which are played similarly to finger cymbals and are used in some Turkish-style dances. Wooden spoons for dancing are available from Chandras.com and Hilarysbazaar.com

36. For further reading, HossamRamzy.com has an interesting and informative article describing the relationship between Egyptian dance and music and the call and reply format.

37. From Ramona's interview with Valerie Larkin in Dubin, Ireland in 1997.

38. *Occupational Outlook Handbook 2000-2001*, U.S. Department of Labor. The Bureau of Labor Statistics website is a useful source of data: stats.bls.gov

39. *Wooing and Winning Business* by Spring Asher and Wicke Chambers gives expert advice regarding effective public speaking and making public presentations. In addition, it contains a useful section on how to deal with nervousness (which speech coaches call "communication apprehension"), and this advice also applies to performance jitters and stage fright.

40. *Example 2:* One of my friends and I agreed that a modern Egyptian style dancer showed exceptional talent in a performance we saw. I asked a third friend his opinion. He said, *"She's just another cabaret dancer."* I concluded that the two of us who enjoyed the dance were seeing the skill and technique of the dancer's performance, while our male friend saw a dance stylization which didn't particularly appeal to him.

Example 3: One of my friends took visiting relatives to an Atlanta restaurant to see a belly dance performance. She saw the dancer perform a lovely belly dance in a modern style, while one of her relatives, a devout Christian, speculated that *"this must be the way they danced during the time of Jesus."* Her relative was seeing a reflection of history in a Christian context, while my friend was seeing a modern belly dance in an entertainment context.

41. *Belly Dance Television*, BD-TV.com, Volume 2, interview with Carolena Nerricio, Director of FatChanceBellyDance.

42. *Masters of Movement,* by Rose Eichenbaum.

Beat Analysis:

The Finger Cymbal Dance (aka The Wind Chimes Dance)

Choreography by Ramona for The Gwinnett Belly Dance Group

Image/storyline: Wind chimes are reacting to the breeze, the strength of the wind varies, and so the sounds of the chimes vary. The dancers' finger cymbals reflect the sound of the chimes.

The breeze is soft and gentle, and the chimes are blown in gentle patterns,
Entrance in figure 8 floor pattern with cymbals ringing softly,

then the breeze begins to gust and relax, and the chimes respond,
staccato cymbal accents and four poses with the body,

the strength of the breeze is vacillating from periodic gusts to steady winds, and the chimes are blown in big circles,
hip lifts/arm circles are big and definite, cymbals vary from loud to soft sounds, accents repeat, poses and cymbal accents reflect gusts of wind, hip circle with cymbals ringing,

the breeze flows softly, and then the chimes clang together,
shimmies of hips, shoulders and then both together, clap and body wave combination,

the wind is steady, then starts to gust strongly,
hip slides at an even tempo, double hip pushes as accents, cymbal accents accompanying hips,

later becoming a gentle breeze, and the chimes react,

then hip shimmy walking backward with softly ringing cymbals,

the breeze is steady and regular, then becomes irregular and the chimes clang at different times,
group forms two parallel lines, then call and response of dancers' cymbals between the groups,

the strength of the breeze is vacillating from periodic gusts to steady winds,
hip lift sequence repeats, ends by forming a circle, linking cymbals (cymbals are silent),

there is a calm before the storm,
group moves in a circular floor pattern, using the grapevine step,

the eye of the storm: strong winds toss the individual chimes in circles and random patterns,
ripple: each dancer spins in a circle, then improvises a movement,

the storm continues, and the winds come in spurts,
trios take turns performing their choreographed mini-dances,

and the wind retreats, the storm is over, the chimes are quiet.
duets and trios form their poses for the ending, hold poses and accept applause.

The Finger Cymbal Dance (aka The Wind Chimes Dance)

Section	Music	Choreographic Phrase	Cymbals	Floor Pattern
Intro	Fast & soft instrumental	Prepare, then enter stage with cymbals ringing Accents: arms up/4 poses (chorus sings) Hip slides	soft ringing/hands vibrate 3's= RLR+ hesitation Running 8's (2x)	Figure 8 Center stage In place
A	Vocals	R,L Basic hip lifts + arm circle (4x) Accents: torso X (4x)	3's (2x) + ring (8 cts) 3's with pauses	In place —
B	Vocals continue	Hip circle (8cts) Shimmies: hips (8cts), shoulders (8), both (8) Clap & body wave combination (4x, RLRL) Accents: torso X (4x) Hip slides Double hip pushes walking fwd (8 cts x2) Shimmy walking bwd (8 cts)	Ringing softly Ringing softly Clap 2x front/back/side 3's with pauses Running 8's (2x) Double accents with zils Ringing	— — — Diagonal Figure 8 Backward
C	Chorus—softer Vocal	Group forms 2 parallel lines (8 cts x 4) Cymbals call & respond	3's Call & response	Group in 2 lines —
A	Instrumental Vocals-soft	R,L Basic hip lifts + arm circle (4x) Accents: torso X (4x)	3's (2x) + ring (8 cts) 3's with pauses	Group forms circle In place
D	Vocals—soft	Circle travels—grapevine step (8 cts x3)	Cymbals/hands connected	Circle
E	Instrumental—soft	Ripple: each dancer spins then improvises Trios perform their mini-dances Trios form scattered poses—ending Hold poses & accept applause	Improvised Cymbals optional — —	Circle Half circle Scattered —

Choreography by Ramona (2006)   Costume style suggestions: Bellydance cabaret, tribal fusion or ethnic dress

NOTE: This choreography works with multiple song selections by adapting the pacing of the movements. When using a specific song, I list the CD, name of song & length of track on class notes so that students can purchase the CD for home practice.

Resources and bibliography

Check out public libraries, interlibrary loan, and used booksellers for out-of-print titles. Due to space limitations, this list is incomplete—there are many other helpful resources available!

Discount books, music, and DVDs:

Amazon.com (new and used books, music, DVDs)
Half.com (used and new books, music, DVDs)
Bookfinder.com (new, used and rare books, price comparisons)

Belly dance books:

Art of Belly Dance, (book/CD/DVD/cymbal/ jewel set) by Carolena Nericcio (FCBD.com)
Bellydance, by Dolphina
Bellydance, by Keti Sharif
Bellydancing, (book/CD set) by Rania Bossonis
Bellydancing Basics, by Laura Cooper
Bellydancing, The Sensual Art of Energy and Spirit, by Pina Coluccia et al.
Bellydancing for Fitness, by Tamalyn Dallal
Belly Dance, the Dance of the Mother Earth, by Tina Hobin
Grandmother's Secrets: The Ancient Rituals and Healing Power of Belly Dancing, by Rosina-Fawzia B. Al-Rawi, Monique Arav (Translator)
Quality of Belly Dance, (encyclopedia of bellydance moves) by Veda Sireem (vedasereem.com)
Serpent of the Nile: Women and Dance in the Arab World, by Wendy Buonaventura
The Belly Dance Book, edited by Tazz Richards
The Tribal Bible, (American Tribal Style Bellydance) by Kajira Djoumahna (Blacksheepbellydance.com)

Belly dance periodicals:

Belly Dance Television, BD-TV.com, a DVD periodical
The Chronicles Magazine, Isisandthestardancers.com
Habibi Magazine, Habibimagazine.com

Business books:

A Dancer's Manual, a Motivational Guide to Professional Dancing, by Bobby Boling
Dancing . . . For a Living, by Don Mirault
The Super Studio: The Guide to a Successful Dance Studio, by Debbie Roberts
Wooing and Winning Business, (public speaking) by Spring Asher and Wicke Chambers
You Can Make Money From Your Hobby, (Christian business book) by Martha Pullen, Ph.D.

Books for cross-training:

The Art of Teaching Dance Technique, by Joan Schlaich and Betty Dupont
Anatomy and Kinesiology for Ballet Teachers, by Eivind Thomasen and Rachel-Anne Rist
Ancient Egyptian Dances, by Irena Lexova (1935; reprinted 2000)
Bullet-Proof Abs: 2nd Edition of Beyond Crunches, by Pavel Tsatsouline
Connections, by Gabrielle Roth
Dance and the specific image: Improvisation, by Daniel Nagrin
Every Little Movement, (about Delsarte Theory) by Ted Shawn (1954; reprinted 1963, 1974)
How to Dance Forever, (taking care of your body) by Daniel Nagrin
Jump into Jazz, by Minda Goodman Kraines and Esther Pryor
Mastery, by George Leonard
Meditation as Medicine, (yoga meditation) by Dharma Singh Khalsa, M.D. and Cameron Stauth
Relax into Stretch, by Pavel Tsatsouline
Returning to Health, (dance and cancer patients) by Anna Halprin
Sacred Woman, Sacred Dance, by Iris Stewart
Somatics, (healthy movement, gentle exercises) by Thomas Hanna

Choreography technique books:

A Sense of Dance, by Constance A. Schrader
Building Dances, (book/card set) by Susan McGreevy-Nichols and Helene Scheff
Choreography, by Sandra Minton
Choreography and the Specific Image, by Daniel Nagrin
Dance Composition, by Jacqueline Smith
Masters of Movement, (interviews with choreographers) by Rose Eichenbaum
The Six Questions: Acting Technique for Dancers, by Daniel Nagrin

Cultural aspects of dance:

A Trade Like Any Other: Female Singers and Dancers in Egypt, by Karin Van Nieuwkerk
Bodytalk: the Meaning of Human Gestures, by Desmond Morris
Choreophobia Solo Improvised Dance in the Iranian World, by Anthony Shay (mazdapub.com)
Dances of Ecstacy, DVD
Daughter of Egypt, Farida Fahmy and the Reda Troupe, by Marjorie Franken (fahmydaughterofegypt.bizland.com)
Flute of Sand: Experiences with the Mysterious Ouled Nail, by Lawrence Morgan (1956) reprinted edition available, email Wendy@buonaventura.com for information
Images of Enchantment, Visual and Performing Arts of the Middle East, edited by Sherifa Zuhur
Keeping Together in Time, Dance and Drill in Human History, by William McNeill
Middle Eastern Dance, by Penni AlZayer
Satin Rouge, DVD comedy-drama about belly dancers in Tunisia
Something in the Way She Moves, (U.K. title: *I Put a Spell on You*), by Wendy Buonaventura
The Romany Trail, Gypsy Music in Africa, DVD
World History of the Dance, by Curt Sachs (1937)

Facial expression:

Emotions Revealed, by Paul Ekman, www.Emotionsrevealed.com
Subtle and Micro Expression Training Tools, CD-ROM (learn to recognize emotions by their associated facial expressions; available at Emotionsrevealed.com)

Stage makeup how-to:

Beauty and the East, by Wendy Buonaventura (Buonaventura.com)
Delilah's Costume Video, by Delilah (Visionarydance.com)
Face Forward, and all other books by Kevyn Aucoin (widely available at bookstores and libraries)
Face It, video by Meleah, in-depth belly dance makeup how-to (Meleah.com)
MAC Cosmetics stores and *Maccosmetics.com* for professional makeup advice and shopping.

Music education books and recordings:

25 Essential Rhythms, CD by Uncle Mafufo (Unclemafufo.com)
Doumbek Delight, Mastering Finger Cymbals, Arabic Tambourine, (books and companion recordings) by Mary Ellen Donald (Maryellendonald.com)
Ear Training for the Body, by Katherine Teck
Effortless Mastery, (book/CD set), by Kenny Werner
Making Music in the Arab World: The Culture and Artistry of Tarab, by A.J. Racy
Playing Finger Cymbals with Jamila, CD (Suhaila.com)
Inner Game of Music, by Barry Green with W. Timothy Gallway
The Voice of Egypt: Umm Kulthum, Arabic Song, and Egyptian Society in the Twentieth Century, book by Virginia Danielson (video also available)
The Music of the Arabs, book by Habib Hassan Toouma (CD also available)
When the Women Were Drummers: A Spiritual History of Rhythm, book by Layne Redmond (also music and instructional recordings at Layneredmond.com)
Zils! Intermediate to Advanced, DVD (Zhelene.com)

Sources for belly dance supplies, props, DVDs, CDs, retreats and more.
Space does not permit listing all sources. The following are a few favorites:

Aspyn's Closet, Custom bellydance costumes, email Elizabethallison@hotmail.com for info.
BellydanceSuperstars.com, Online catalogue, performance schedule and more.

DelphiDance.com, Tribal fusion classes and more. Shop at the Lawrenceville, Georgia store.

DynamicBellyDance.com, Ramona's website

FCBD.com, FatChanceBellydance online catalogue, American Tribal Style classes and more.

Faye4u.com, Originales by Faye, costumes and more

HilarysBazaar.com, Hilary's Bazaar, order online or shop at the Edinburgh, Scotland store.

HossamRamzy.com, CDs, DVD, and informative articles about Egyptian dance.

OasisDanceCamp.com, Oasis Dance Camp retreats featuring instructor Cassandra.

Suhaila.com, Online catalogue, newsletter, classes and more.

TurquoiseIntl.com, Turquoise International catalogue.

VisionaryDance.com, Online catalogue, retreats, classes and more.

Selected websites for further reading about belly dance:

Bhuz.com
DynamicBellyDance.com
Gildedserpent.com
Learn-to-belly-dance.com
Shira.net
Suhaila.com
Tribe.net
VisionaryDance.com

Belly dance costume supplies and accessories from Hilary's Bazaar (Edinburgh, Scotland).

About the Author

Ramona is a belly dance instructor and scientist in metro Atlanta. Gwinnett County Parks and Recreation Department awarded her "Instructor of the Year," and she has been featured on local television and in the *Atlanta Journal-Constitution* and *Gwinnett Daily Post* newspapers. Ramona began dance training at age five, with a background in a variety of genres, but has always been fascinated with belly dance.

Ramona has mentored students who are now professional soloists, troupe directors, choreographers and workshop instructors. They perform cabaret belly dance, tribal fusion belly dance and Christian worship dance, performing throughout the southeastern U.S. in a variety of venues ranging from concert stages, restaurants and civic events to churches. Ramona also coaches many passionate amateur dancers.

The Chronicles, Habibi, The Caravan and *Arabesque* dance magazines have published informative articles by Ramona. She has a background in journalism and technical writing, and was an editor of an entertainment magazine and university women's periodical in the 1980's.

A graduate of Marshall University with degrees in Psychology and Geology, she works as an environmental scientist, specializing in reviewing and writing technical documents, and participating in workgroups for projects with complex environmental issues. She teaches belly dance in addition to being a wife and mother in metro Atlanta.

How to contact the author

Your comments and thoughts about this book are welcomed. Visit Ramona's website at DynamicBellyDance.com or email

Ramona@DynamicBellyDance.com

In addition, Ramona teaches group and private classes. Inquiries about her availability for seminars and workshops should be directed to her email address or by writing to:

American Bellydance Innovations
P.O. Box 1083
Atlanta, GA 30301-1083

To order additional copies of

Dynamic BellyDance:

The Joyful Journey of Dancemaking and Performing

as gifts for friends and colleagues, please visit our website for
easy ordering online and secure credit card payments:

www.DynamicBellyDance.com

or send your check (payable to American Bellydance Innovations) to:

American Bellydance Innovations
P.O. Box 1083
Atlanta, GA 30301-1083

The book price is $40.00 each.
Please add $5.00 shipping and handling for one book,
and $2.50 for each additional book.

Georgia residents add applicable sales tax.

Foreign orders, please pay by credit card.

Email: Ramona@DynamicBellyDance.com